The Greek-o-File
Volume I

written & edited by
Sylvia & Terry Cook

The Greek-o-File Volume I: published in Great Britain by Greek-o-File Ltd 2002
Copyright © Greek-o-File™ November 2002

ISBN 0-9543593-0-5

The **Greek-o-File Vol I** is a compendium of articles and anecdotes written by Sylvia & Terry Cook and the many contributors acknowledged with their work. Illustrations and photographs were supplied by authors of the relevant articles except where specified.

Edited and set: Sylvia Cook

Acknowledgements

Without the enthusiasm of subscribers to the quarterly Greek-o-File magazines since late 1998, and their contributions submitted over the years, we could not have contemplated producing this first Greek-o-File book. Though in a new format, the book follows a similar style of content, now aimed at a wider market through book stores, but we still depend on and thank those who continue to support us as direct subscribers and contributors. Thanks especially to the contributors to this book.

We thank our regular advertisers and supporters, many since the early days of Greek-o-File, who have encouraged us as promoters of a product (the real Greece) which they too believe in, as much as for commercial reasons. Most of them also advertise in these pages.

Maps are an important part of travel notes and understanding the layout of a region. We are indebted to both Road Editions and Efstathiadis for their kind permission to reproduce and adapt their maps where specified.

We are very grateful to the London Greek Embassy Press Office for their continuing support and to the AG Leventis Foundation.

Printed by: Cox & Wyman Ltd, Reading, Berkshire, UK

Greek-o-File Ltd, UK
Email: mail@greekofile.co.uk,
Website: www.greekofile.co.uk

Greek-o-File Vol. I - Contents

Introduction

The Greek-o-File Vol. I is a compendium of articles and anecdotes written by and for people who love the Greece of the Greeks.

It is not for those who revel in the noisy touristy places that could be any-where in the world, nor for those who expect to find everything English with sunshine when they go abroad, but it is for those who have been captivated by the differences of Greece - the friendly welcome of the locals, the quiet unspoilt villages and resorts, the beauty of coast and countryside and the rich past which seems evident all around. Whether you have a favourite place or places you keep returning to, or you enjoy exploring new parts of Greece, or you want to know what it is about Greece that makes others keep returning, The Greek-o-File will put you in the picture.

In these illustrated pages you will find articles to inform and to entertain you, to give you ideas for places to visit, to help you appreciate the background and lives of the Greek people, to relive your holiday memories through the anecdotes of others or to help you plan your future in Greece.

The style is based on our earlier Greek-o-File quarterly publications which built into a FILE on all things Greek (back issues available for newcomers to Greek-o-File), but in this book format we have more flexibility and have added new sections and more useful information.

It is a book to dip into, or to read from cover to cover AND to retain for reference. The style is personal and varied, rather than polished - it reflects the experiences and interest of real people; people like you.

We hope you enjoy reading this collection of experiences in Greece and information on all things Greek and perhaps send your contributions for consideration for our next volume.

Sylvia Cook

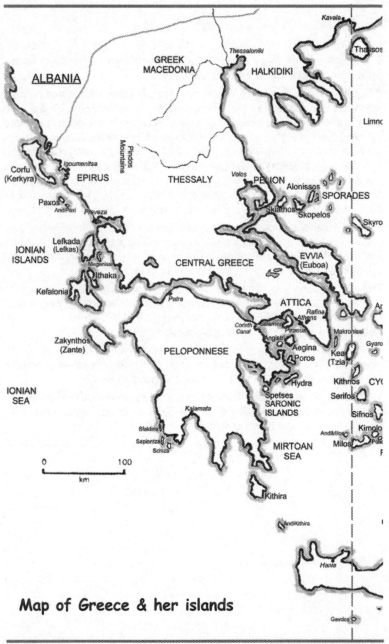

Map of Greece & her islands

Travel Notes

Poros Profile *by Sylvia Cook*

Poros (Πόρος), is in the Saronic group of islands between Athens and the Methana peninsula of the Peloponnese. It is made up of two road-connected islands, the larger northern island of **Kalavria** (Καλαύρεια) and the main town island of **Sphairia** (Σφαιρειά), totalling just 28 sq kms. The latter is separated from the Peloponnese town of **Galatas** (Γαλατάς) by a narrow half kilometre wide sound. Administratively, Poros is linked with the Peloponnese area around Galatas, **Trizina** (Τροιζήνα) and the lemon groves of **Lemonodasos** (Λεμονοδάσος).

The northern island is green with inland pine woodlands and fertile coastal areas where local inhabitants farm and fish for a living. The beaches and proximity to Athens draw many visitors, so tourism has become a major occupation. Hotels, shops, tavernas and bars are mostly situated along the south coast and on the smaller island, in Poros Town.

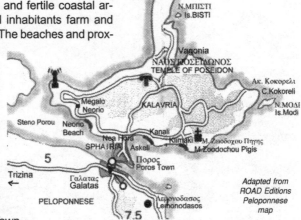

Adapted from ROAD Editions Peloponnese map

Poros Background

❏ *There was a Mycenaean settlement on Poros at the site which became the Sanctuary of Poseidon in the 6th c. BC. The sanctuary was the centre for the ancient Kalavrian league and a refuge for the persecuted.*

❏ *After the Roman period the ancient city was abandoned. The modern town on its current site was first built in Medieval times.*

❏ *The Naval college on Poros, near where the canal separates the two islands, was the principal naval base in south eastern Greece in the 18th and 19th centuries and is still responsible for the training of many Greek naval cadets today.*

❏ *The 18th century monastery, Zoodochou Pigis, is open for visitors and there is also a small archaeological museum in Poros town.*

Poros Perambulation *by Gerry Brown*

Even though it was mid September a booking was necessary on the Flying Dolphin from **Piraeus**. The fare was about €12.00 and the journey, in quite choppy seas, took just over an hour to the Saronic island of **Poros** (Πόρος).

It is only on arrival at Poros that the first time visitor begins to appreciate the geography of the area. To get an aerial geographical overview of the whole province an early visit to the Posidion restaurant/bar atop a mountain behind **Kanali** (Κανάλι) is recommended if only for this photo opportunity. From the port take the left fork at the filling station at Kanali and follow the excellent road that winds for about 4kms up the hill to the Posidion. There is no entry charge during the day, although drinks are a bit expensive, but from a terrace table the fantastic views are well worth the time and cost.

The beaches and tourist accommodation are mainly along the south coast of Kalavria set into the coves to the west of the causeway and the rather more lively broader strands to the east. The majority of the island's restaurants and bars are gathered around the port, and a fine and diverse choice they are. Of course there are the usual harbourside joints where touts try to entice you into their establishments but there are also many good value family run tavernas serving Greek and non-Greek meals.

Unfortunately the kafeneion seems to have all but disappeared. In fact the old tin-topped-tabled bar with wooden chairs is now more likely to be an internet café with glass coffee tables, chromium seats and earnest young Scandinavians with zeppelin sized rucksacks and acne.

We stayed at the Saga Hotel in **Kanali**, found on a Poros website. Here a note of warning. On the same site was accommodation listed as 'Villa Eucalyptus', our first choice had it not been closed in September. What an escape! An Estate Agent trying to sell a decrepit ruin of a garden shed on Beirut dockside would have a hard job to surpass the flowery description and images given for the 'Villa Eucalyptus' we saw.

The Saga hotel was a splendid modern hotel run by Takis and Zefi Alexandropoulos and their young family, named as the ancient Norse for *'long story'* in the hope it would go on forever. Here and at a few other hotels/apartments that we visited, is the reassuring manifestation that at least some Greek hoteliers are bringing their facilities into line with those offered elsewhere in Europe. It could be said that, in terms of room standards, they are now looking at the competition from the Spanish Costas rather than just their cousin Costas. We even had a jacuzzi in our bathroom!

The road network of Poros closely resembles the lower case Greek letter 'φ'. There is a scenic road around the coast bisected by a link road from the north of Kalavria, across the causeway and down to the port. Motor scooter hire is a good way to cover the 25km or so of asphalt road.

To explore the main island of **Kalavria** we started by heading west from Kanali, where the Greek Naval College is and where most of the narrow beach is taken by fishing caiques. The road on the land side has many low-rise apartment buildings and several tavernas as well as motorbike and motor boat *(see later)* hire offices. After a couple of clicks the bays of **Micro Neorio** (Μικρό Νεώριο) and **Megalo Neorio** (Μεγάλο Νεώριο) are reached. These self explanatory stretches of fine but gritty, white sand have good facilities. Beach furniture is available and there are the usual large fronted restaurants, complete with faded photographs of dishes on offer. Has anyone else noticed that these images bear the same lack of realism to the

Megalo Neorio Beach

actual product that is also found as 'serving suggestions' on the packaging of frozen ready meals? Megalo Neorio also has water activities for the young and fit, mainly involving fibreglass boats with high powered engines.

The road continues past **Love Bay**, which is more of a sheltered cove with a kantina, to **Russian Bay** where once the Tsar's navy assembled to assist the Greeks in the war of independence against the Turks. On the day of our visit (and who will forget the 11th September 2001), work had started on a new development planned to assimilate some of the remaining 19th century buildings into a new beach complex. Throughout the 8km journey along the southern coast road one is always aware of the vast expanse of lemon tree groves across the water on the mainland slopes of **Lemonodasos** (λεμονοδάσος) and **Trizina**. I have it on good authority that in spring the scent of the blossom carries across the sound to Poros.

As the road turns to the north and loses its asphalt, it rises from sea level to give glorious views over **Steno Porou** (Στενό Πόρου), the busy channel used by the ferries and Dolphins coming and going to Athens. The track, which is fine for four wheels and passable with care for those on two, meanders through green forests and ravines for about 5km to the farming area known as **Fousa** (Φουσα) where the asphalt restarts. There are plenty of direction signs to the ruins of the **Sanctuary of Poseidon** but unfortunately little on-site information other than the single A4 page at the entrance. As befits the god of the sea, the temple overlooks the Aegean to Athens in the far distance, recognisable by the horizon sandwich of blue sea, white buildings, brown smog and blue sky. The site is some 100m by 200m and was excavated by Swedish archaeologists in 1894 and latterly by the Germans during their occupation in 1944. In our view it has fortunately been left in a similar condition to what Knossos must have been like before Mr Evans' tacky reconstructions. For a break from culture backtrack a couple of hundred metres from the temple to a signed junction for **Vagionia** (Βαγιονιά) and follow the descending track to its bay where there is a beautiful beach, clear safe bathing and a seasonal kantina.

The 5km of good road through the wooded eastern centre of Kalavria leads back to the south coast at **Klimaki** (Κλιμάκι) where a left turn is recommended to visit the inhabited **Monastery of Zoodochos Pigi** (Ζωοδόχος Πιγή). Suitably dressed visitors are allowed to enter certain areas including the impressive *iconostasis*, the highly decorated altar screen. The 100m

wide beach a short distance below the monastery is a well-integrated amenity and an ideal example of how Greek resorts can exploit their natural attractions without ruining the reason for their popularity. The sand is fine and white, the sea is safe and clean, the three on-the-beach tavernas have excellent facilities and menus and there is plenty of unobtrusive parking.

The final section of the road loops around Kalavria, passes the wider beaches of **Askeli** (Ασκέλι) where a lot of the night life is to be found, and ends at **Kanali** where the causeway crosses to the port island of **Sphairia**. On the seaward side of the road, which has one way traffic during the high season, are the quays for the ferries, Mega and Flying Dolphins, slipper boats to **Galatas** and water taxis. The opposite side of the road is a contiguous kilometre of restaurants, tavernas, gift shops and travel agencies. The sheer quantity of roadside seating together with the delightful *platias* of Hero Square and St. George's Square elevate the weekend *volta* to an Olympian event. Behind this façade is the old town with its famous clock tower, unfortunately hidden by tarpaulin and scaffolding on our visit. Here you find the typical Greek narrow alleyways and steps with the more indigenous shops and tavernas.

There are several frequent water taxis to use for the short trip across the sound to the mainland, but we decided to hire our own self-drive 4-5 seater motor boat that cost €14.66 for the day and an extra €5.90 for the fuel. With this, quite speedy, mode of transport we were able to visit the distant Peloponnese shores of **Trizina** stopping off at the townships of **Dami** and **Bidi** where there are a couple of small isolated

Gerry & Jane in Motor Boat, Trizina coast

beach complexes with mooring for water taxis. From either of these landfalls it is less than a half hour walk to the ancient town of **Troizen** (Τροίζεν) the birthplace of Theseus, later to achieve his moment of fame by slaying the Minotaur and escaping from the labyrinth with a little help from Ariadne's sewing basket. Troizen has developed into the modern town of **Trizina** from which the area takes its name. There are still plenty of disassembled stones around the town, to keep the history seekers happy, including the remains of one of the first Byzantine churches in the Aegean. Besides the archaeology and protected wildlife in the locality there is the 'Devil's Gorge', a conduit for the mountain rainfall, but hardly more than a bridged dry ravine without the water.

To those familiar with Newcastle and Gateshead or Liverpool and Birkenhead the relationship of Poros to Galatas will be well understood. The bigger, brasher neighbour across the river/sound tends to patronise the lesser attractions of its twin but just like its English counterparts Galatas has a lot to offer if only in terms of cheaper accommodation and some shops that do not sell dubious ceramics, beach accessories and trinkets. At Galatas and at the quaysides of Poros the visitor in a motor boat should be careful to avoid mooring at a ferry landing but providing common courtesies are observed, particularly when 'mooring off', there are plenty of parking places.

Generally we were very impressed by Poros and because we went on to visit a couple of islands in the Cyclades this gave us a good opportunity for making comparisons. Drinking on Poros was cheaper, the quality and choice of food was better and the accommodation was less expensive. On this last subject we had a pleasant conversation with our well-travelled hosts, Zefi and Takis, during which I chided them about Poros being the Brighton of Athens. Yes, they admitted, at weekends very few of the couples were actually Kyrios and Kyria but it is these Athenians who demand the better facilities that benefit the Alexandropoulos' target clients from northern Europe.

We could find no locally published guide to Poros so before finishing we must thank an old school friend who now lives there. We bumped into Mike in a bar on Poros and the couple of hangovers were well worth his advice and company during our stay.

Finally we travelled back from Poros by taking the Spetses to Piraeus ferry that also calls in at Methana and Aegina during the two hour journey to the bustle of Piraeus harbour.

How to get to Poros

By Air - to Athens, (or charter to Kalamata) then road and ferry.

By Sea - ferries from Piraeus, also Aegina, Hydra, Methana, Spetses, or short hop from Galatas or Porto Heli & Ermioni, Peloponnese.

A Walk Through the Samaria Gorge *by Vivien Powell*

Here is Vivien's account of walking through the most famous of many gorges that cut through the mountains of Crete. It is a unique experience which many visitors to Crete try to fit into their holiday - but not for the fainthearted or unfit!

Sketchmap by Sylvia Cook

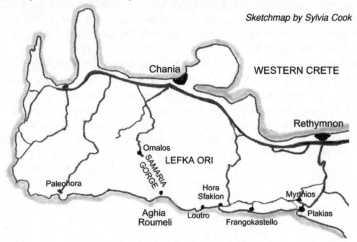

The Samaria Gorge in southwest Crete is reputedly, at 18km, the longest in Europe. Because of its length and situation, it's difficult to walk independently, unless you go down and back in a day. Camping is not permitted along the route and the only way back to civilisation from the bottom end is by boat. There are many organised trips which drop you at the top and meet you off the boat at the end of the day. I tend to shy away from group activities, preferring to do things away from the crowd, but I really wanted to walk the gorge, so with some reluctance I booked the coach trip from **Plakias** (on the south coast, south of Rethymnon). It was May, soon after the gorge opened to the public after the winter 'rainy season' so I hoped it would not be too crowded. The river can become quite treacherous in winter and the Gorge is closed to the public from November to the end of April.

On the day of the trip I get up before dawn, the stars still twinkling and a sliver of a silver moon still high in the cloudless black sky. As I walk to the coach, the pale morning sun creeps up over the mountains, lighting up the sky, reflecting starkly off the white harbour-moored boats and the seafront tavernas of the still-sleeping village. Frothing white waves break against the sandy shore from a clear, turquoise blue sea.

Out of Plakias, heading north through the awesome, rocky gorge of **Kourtaliotiko**, the sun climbs higher, painting the mountain tops rich orange. I catch sight of a village nestling way up in the hills and imagine its inhabitants gradually gathering at the simple *kafeneion* for their first *kafe Elliniko* of the day.

We take the main road via **Rethymnon** to **Chania** and beyond, the high peaks of the **Lefka Ori** still clad in patches of snow, gleaming atop the sun-bathed mountains in the clear morning light to our left, and to our right the Cretan Sea like a sapphire lake below us. The vista changes as more and more trees line the roadside and march up the foothills of the mountains, sunlight shafting through their branches. Next the mountain road to **Omalos**, the last village before the gorge, winding steeply ever upwards, looking down into wooded valleys and away to the sea. After a breakfast of *tiropitta* and black Nescafe, and buying a large sandwich and a bottle of water for later, I rejoin the coach for the further 5 minutes drive to the beginning of the gorge, high, high in the mountain tops, with breathtaking scenery over the pine trees to the highest snow-clad peak.

The descent on foot begins via a kind of winding staircase - a stony affair constructed of wood, with rustic wooden handrail - that twists and turns and is quite steep. Many coach parties have deposited their passengers here

and it is quite noisy with the sound of other tourists' voices. After half an hour I begin to wonder if I will have any peace to absorb the sights, sounds and smells of this beautiful place, but eventually, being quicker than many, I find myself alone on the stony track, the scent of pine needles in my nose, the twittering of birds in the trees, and rocks and wild flowers on all sides. As I descend, the mountains begin to tower above me.

The authorities have considerately placed resting places by natural springs en route with benches for walkers to rest their feet a while. I stop at the second of these, quenching my thirst with natural spring water and absorbing the peacefulness.

Now the path levels off a little amongst the tall pine trees, but is still very rocky with many loose pebbles. I stop to take in the view, looking up at orange rocks striped with black and dotted with shrubs and wild flowers in yellow and pink.

The next stop has a 'loo' in a wooden hut - a ceramic hole in the ground with footrests either side. I make use of the facilities, then make a small detour to explore the wildlife - huge crimson dragon arums and clumps of tiny whitish-pink cyclamen nestling in the roots of giant cypress trees. Back on the track, around the next bend is a tiny stone church - still in use. Inside is an altar with icons, a large candle and the smell of incense and earth.

The sound of water becomes louder, competing with the birds and drowning out human voices, which have lessened anyway as people become weary and save their energy to concentrate on their sure-footedness. Eventually, I arrive at the first river crossing, water tumbling over orange and white boulders, frothing into pools of pale turquoise. As the path meanders up, down, back and forth, it crosses the river many times, each one more spectacular than the last; orange cliffs dipping their feet into the cool river and tree branches casting patterns on the huge white rocks. Often the river has to be crossed via stepping stones.

By one o'clock I'm beginning to get peckish. Around the next bend I see a wooden footbridge over the river, leading to the old settlement of Samaria.

Some beautiful new houses are being built here, deep in the heart of the gorge, to rehouse the old inhabitants relocated in 1962 when this National Park was first created. Beneath a fig tree I find a bench that is not crowded, and eat most of my ham and cheese roll and apple, swig yet more spring water, and sit back to rest and people-watch for a while.

A Greek man I'd noticed earlier with some other people walks into a nearby house and out again; handsome, swarthy with black beard. Just as I'm preparing to resume my walk, suitably refreshed and relieved in another ceramic loo-hole, the man leads out two brown donkeys right in front of me, then mounts the first one and sets off, leading the other on a rope. Their pace is similar, on the whole, to mine, the donkeys' hooves having some difficulty over the rocky terrain. Keeping a respectful distance behind, I decide to use them as my pacemakers for a while. There's no-one else in sight - just the Greek and his donkeys tip-tapping along, and me walking behind at a steady pace through the most peaceful, magical part of the whole walk. A mostly level, pine-needle carpeted path through tall trees, the river gurgling to the right below and birds singing happily in the treetops. I feel that wonderful at-one-with-nature, heart-thrilling stillness that you only get in the great outdoors; a 'here-and-now, nothing-else-matters' moment.

The path suddenly changes into very stony, rocky terrain. At a wide part of the river with huge stepping-stones, the donkey-man stops to let the animals drink, and I have to wait before I can cross. There are other walkers on the opposite bank and we begin to traverse a wide area of grey, shale-like stones. I guess the people of Samaria used this area to provide stones for house building. It's difficult underfoot - a bit like walking on Brighton Beach. The path narrows again, with boulders and smaller rocks on each side. I'm really in my stride now but the track closely follows the edge of the river here and is not really distinguishable as a path - I'm jumping from rock to rock like a true Capricorn! A woman in front of me hails the donkey-man and round the next river bend I see the reason - a limping woman with a bandaged knee. The bearded Greek dismounts and helps the woman into the saddle. I pass and continue over yet more slippery step-

The Iron Gates (in October with less water)

ping stones and up the path on the opposite side.

The next resting place is in a level valley with many trees under towering orange cliffs. I find a flat stone beneath a young tree and lean back against its trunk to rest awhile. The burdened donkeys reappear, led by the Greek. The woman's partner mounts the other donkey and they continue on their way.

From this green oasis the path narrows again and the mountain sides close in. The rock formations are spectacular - great crevices and caves high up in the mountainsides, with the river down below, rushing along in its hurry to reach the sea. I reach the narrowest point - the 'Iron Gates' - along with a few others. The river is deep here and a wooden walkway has been erected to keep our feet dry. The mountains on either side of the rushing river almost touch at this point, the rock faces rising sheer to the sky, which has become cloudy now, providing some respite from the sun and perfect walking conditions.

Once through the 'Iron Gates' the river widens out and the path follows it, crossing and recrossing it, sometimes via stepping stones, sometimes little wooden plank footbridges. The terrain is becoming level and much easier. After a while the whole valley widens out and I catch a glimpse of the sea in the distance. I pass through the **old** village of **Aghia Roumeli**, tempted by the offers of ice cream or orange juice, but decide to hang on. I pass a gleaming white church, a few houses with gardens full of orange, lemon and apricot trees and wild hollyhocks. Finally I arrive at **Aghia Roumeli** by the sea. My tired feet are urging me to paddle in the cool water, but it's cloudy and windy now, the sand is black and pebbly and the thought of a cold beer in a taverna quickly silences the urgings of my feet. I choose a comfortable seat, looking out over the sea, order a *mikri bira* and watch the people boarding boats.

No words can really describe this walk. It's nature at its best - awesome, magical and wonderful. But I decide to try, to put pen to paper and write this account for my friend back at Plakias who could not undertake such a walk. I have two hours until my boat leaves, the last of the day to Hora Sfakion where the coach will be waiting to drive us back.

After a second beer and pleasant chat to the waiter, practising my Greek, the sun comes out and I spend half an hour lazing on the beach, boots and socks removed, basking in the warmth of the sun, my achievement of the day and warm contentment. Then a stroll to the taverna where we'd prearranged to collect our boat tickets. I drink a sludgy Greek coffee. The boat arrives, just 15 minutes late. I sit on the top deck on the landward side to watch the coast in the evening sun, but as we pick up speed the wind in my face takes my breath away and I move to the middle deck and stand astern watching the patterns of the froth from the wake, the long rays of the evening sun catching the waves and colouring the coastline's hills. We stop at **Loutro**, a tiny village with no roads, that spills from the hillsides into the harbour, all the buildings painted white and blue, adults and children waving from the harbourside tavernas.

At **Hora Sfakion** we disembark - only an hour from Aghia Roumeli - and find our coach amongst the many waiting there. Our journey back takes us through tiny villages, treacherous winding lanes, across a bridge, through **Frangocastello** past its famous haunted fort. The sun finally sets and darkness enfolds us. I catch a glimpse of Plakias twinkling away by the sea as we crawl slowly up a dusty road to **Sellia**, driving it seems across its rooftops, then on to **Mirthios** and down the winding road to **Plakias**.

My friend greets me with a huge hug and a newly opened bottle of wine. By 9.30pm the solar heated water is none too hot, but my shower seems the best ever, cleaning the white dust from every pore. We walk to the taverna to eat - everything just as it was yesterday, except that inside me something's changed. I don't think my first walk in the Samaria Gorge will be my last, but it may well be the best.

Hospitality - Just One More ... *by Cliff Nye*

We were staying in Parga at the Rezi Hotel, a very nice cosy, family run business. During our stay we had decided to try to do a lot of walking around the area. One day at about 9.30am we set off after breakfast for the village of Aghia (Αγια) about 11kms to the north, seemingly in the middle of nowhere.

The walk was fairly uneventful; beautiful scenery, many olive groves, we spotted a few birds of prey and a couple of castles. One of the castles, we heard, had been occupied by Ali Pasha, but we did not know which one as there seemed to be many with the same name.

We arrived in Aghia about 11.30am and looked around the very sleepy village. There were not that many houses or cottages, but the usual churches, kafeneions and a couple of bars were there to serve the villagers and occasional visitors. Walking past one bar the man who seemed to be the owner called out *'You English?'* We replied *'Yes'* and he beckoned us inside. It was a little early for a drink we thought, but not wanting to get off on the wrong foot agreed to a beer and Coca Cola.

These were brought to our table after a couple of minutes then our host disappeared into his kitchen. We heard much banging and rattling of pots, then after about 10 minutes he appeared again with a plate of roast pork pieces and a small Greek salad. We said we had not ordered food, but he said it was to accompany the drinks.

A little later another Greek gentleman walked in, said *'Good Morning'* to us and also to the owner. He exchanged a few words in Greek with the owner who again went into his kitchen and reappeared with two ouzos. We tried again to say we had not ordered these, but were told that the new arrival had bought them for us. We thanked the man and enjoyed his hospitality. Meanwhile the owner was in the kitchen once more, reappearing with two pears *'for the ouzo'*.

Shortly after another man came in with his wife and in a very English voice said *'Good morning'* to us. We got into conversation and he told us they were from Sheffield (our home town) and were teaching English at the school in Aghia. They also gave private tuition in the evenings. The wife had taught in Sheffield before, at Myers Grove School. What a coincidence - the school is just 50 yards from our house! Of course this led to many more ouzos and each time we received more food; boiled eggs, more pork, more salad, yoghurt and honey, more ouzo, etc.

When we finally tried to leave we were all 'fairly happy'. I said to Christine, my wife, that I was not looking forward to the bill. Another ouzo later I asked the owner for the bill. He looked at us, smiled and said *'1,000 drachma'*. We could not believe the generosity of this man. He was a marvellous host who could only speak three or four words of English and us no Greek, but he was just pleased that we had stayed and had a drink or three. The

English chap asked if we would like a lift back. We declined as he was hardly in a fit state to find his car, let alone drive it.

'Still Life' photos by Sylvia Cook

We finally left at 4.30pm and walked home with such wonderful memories of an unforgettable afternoon. Incidentally, they told us they were due to go out on a wolf hunt the following morning - somehow we don't think so!

They probably did go on a wolf hunt the next day - haven't you noticed how the Greeks seem more resilient than us to the effects of alcohol, often getting up after only a few hours sleep for an early morning start at work before the heat of the day. Perhaps it's all the practice they get. Ed.

Profile of Lefkada *by Sylvia Cook*

Attached to mainland Greece by a narrow causeway and bridge, the enchanting 'island' of **Lefkada** (Λευκάδα) or **Lefkas** is the fourth largest of the Ionian Islands at about 300 sq kms. It lies between Paxos and Kefalonia / Ithaki in the Ionian Sea, Administratively Lefkada incorporates 23 other smaller islands, such as Meganissi, the private Onassis island of Skorpios, Kalamos, Katsos and others mostly in the lagoon which separates the island from mainland Greece.

Lefkada is quiet and beautiful. The least commercialised of the larger Ionian islands, although it does have one or two more lively resorts. Lefkada means 'whiteness'. The pale, almost white, fine sandy beaches on the western coast create the most incredible turquoise shades of sea colour imaginable. The eastern coast is more rocky or with pebble beaches. Inland are small villages amidst farms on green hillsides fed by springs, with the highest peaks in the centre of the island, rising over 1100 metres.

Lefkada is served by good road links around the island and to the mainland and also frequent ferry connections to the southern Ionian islands.

Lefkada Background

❏ *There were settlements in Lefkada during the Neolithic period 4,000BC. Minoan and Achaean artefacts have been found there. One theory put forward by the German, W.Dorpfeld, suggests that Lefkada is Homer's Ithaca. Corinthians founded a town at Lefkas in 7th c BC.*

❏ *The lyric poetess Sappho, exiled from the island of Lesvos for her political views, is said to have committed suicide here, hurling herself onto the rocks from a cliff in the south of Lefkada when rejected by Phaeon, the man she loved.*

❏ *The ancient Corinthians first separated Lefkada from the mainland to provide a shipping channel. The sand spits around Lefkas town formed around the Middle Ages,when they created salt beds to harvest salt (for preserving and consumption) then as today.*

❏ *Lefkada was involved in the naval battle of Salamina, the battle of Platea and the Peloponnesian wars and was taken by Philip II of Macedonia in 338BC. From this time on it generally follows the history of nearby Ionian islands, controlled by Byzantines, Venetians, French, British and finally annexed to Greece in 1864.*

Map adapted from Efstathiadis Road Atlas

Lefkada Travels *by Sylvia Cook*

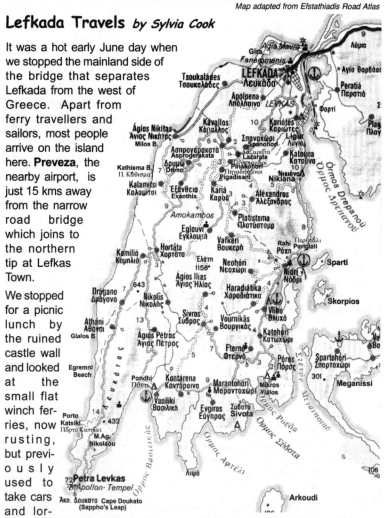

It was a hot early June day when we stopped the mainland side of the bridge that separates Lefkada from the west of Greece. Apart from ferry travellers and sailors, most people arrive on the island here. **Preveza**, the nearby airport, is just 15 kms away from the narrow road bridge which joins to the northern tip at Lefkas Town.

We stopped for a picnic lunch by the ruined castle wall and looked at the small flat winch ferries, now rusting, but previously used to take cars and lor-

ries across to the island. It was very quiet and peaceful here. A narrow drawbridge is opened once every hour (on the hour) to let sailing boats through, but there were very few vehicles waiting for it to reopen.

Lefkas Town awaited the other side, with shallow waters enclosed in a sand spit wall creating a salt-lake haven for water birds to the north. We liked this administrative and commercial capital with its central market paved street and square with shops and cafes around and the 'shanty town' feel in the back streets. The 1953 earthquake left its mark and many repaired houses in the narrow backstreets still had painted corrugated tin or wooden upper walls. Nothing was more than a few storeys high. There were few new buildings and not many hotels here.

The island roads were pretty good and we headed south down the east coast first. Our first stop was **Ligia** (Λυγιά), a fishing village strung out along the main road with rooms and holiday homes in side streets leading down to the sea, but with no beach at this point. However, after the fishing harbour (with fairly large working fishing boats) there was a narrow shingle beach and a paved walkway along the water's edge, passing a few small hotels. Although this was the sea, it seemed more like a lake, being calm and enclosed at one end. We found an out of the way spot to stop for the night near a taverna where we enjoyed a beer. It was a perfect spot to gaze across to the mainland opposite, to a ruined castle but no villages, and down to Ligia harbour.

Later we walked to the harbour and found 2 quiet kafeneions. There was an old man at one so we went in for an ouzo and talked about the fishing boats - they would start work at 6am next day. The man's daughter came back and we talked some more. She told us that Sappho had not thrown herself forwards off the rock, but the accepted way then was to sit in a chair and tip backwards off the cliff. This method was also used to get rid of criminals. If they were lucky enough to survive the fall they were allowed to stay free.

The next day we headed back towards the town then inland to look around the hill villages. The vegetation was thick around here. We stopped to explore **Spanohori** (Σπανοχώρι), where many stone houses had been reno-vated, old ladies dressed in black sat in arch-framed doorways. The butter-flies liked it here too.

Lazarata (Λαζαράτα) was a more modern village on the main road again, but surrounded by yellow gorse hillsides. Soon we were winding down a valley to the west coast with views down to the sea far below. There had been rock falls and maybe we weren't on the road we'd intended, but we

ended up on a good west coast road not far from **Ag. Nikitas** (Αγ. Νικήτας). Parking in the campsite area at the top, we walked down to the tiny white-shingle beach and pale turquoise sea at the end of the steep sided gorge. The resort seemed charismatic, but quite developed for such a small village. I could imagine it could be noisy in high season.

We decided to move on, past **Milos** beach, more easily accessed from the sea, to the larger beach of **Kathisma** (Π. Κάθισμα) where parking would be easier. It was a long beach with sun beds, but well spaced out in a single row so not off-putting. The balcony taverna above had a car park with showers - and many steps down to the white sand and shingle beach below. Of all the 'impossible' shades of blue we've encountered before in Greece, the west coast beaches of Lefkada have to be the prettiest 'most impossible' - from the darkest turquoise of the deep sea, gradually lightening to the shallow creamy pale turquoise waves lapping onto sesame seed-like shingle sand. I was transfixed. This is not a resort, just a day trip beach really, although there are a few rooms available on the cliff top. There is no shade so the tavernas at either end, the kantina in the middle and Balcony taverna we visited above are welcome breaks.

We stayed in the car park that night, as did 2 other motorhomes. It may not be permitted in high season, but they seemed OK about it and we revisited the taverna in the evening, chatting in simple Greek with the friendly owner/waiter, who also spoke good English.

It was a stormy, windy night, but fresh and sunny next morning with large waves crashing onto the beach, adding to the incredible view we looked over again as we sipped our morning 'metrio' coffees.

The next village down the west coast was **Kalamitsi** (Καλαμίτσι), quite bustling with tavernas and rooms, but also old ladies with donkeys and goats. The beach road was steep and winding so we decided to give it a miss in our Grekovan (converted ex-Luton airport minibus). We'd been stuck meeting traffic on too many narrow or steep roads before and our guidebooks implied it was just a quiet beach with no facilities.

The road continued uphill, first through lush vegetation and flowers, later more barren then scrubby again with a few olive trees. **Dragano** (Δράγανο) had lots of newly tiled rooftops and oil and honey for sale. **Athani** (Αθάνι) was soon after with quite a few tavernas and rooms in the village and **Gialos** (Γιαλός) beach below.

The road was still pretty good, although our map implied it should not be. We passed a turning to **Egremni** (Εγκρεμνοί) beach. At the Oasis taverna was pine shaded seating at the junction to Porto Katsiki (5km it said, 6km to Akrotirio) and a viewing point overlooking another white and turquoise beach below - presumably Egremni. We saw new tarmac on the Porto Katsiki road but were not sure about the other one. We tried it anyway - driving southwards with incredible views of the many islands to the east and Kefalonia ahead of us in the distance. The tarmac ran out - roadworkers still working on it. We did want to continue to '**Sappho's Leap**' if possible, so drove to the end of the new road base of chippings and got out to walk a little further south along the track, between flowering shrubs and thyme, accompanied by lots of butterflies. Our maps showed **Lefkatas** and **Cape Doukato** at the end, but local signs referred to **Akrotiri** (meaning just 'cape') - the venue of Sappho's demise. We saw it in the distance, but realised there would be nothing to see there so contented ourselves with this view before turning back to take the road to **Porto Katsiki** (Πόρτο Κατσίκι).

At the end of a misleadingly long road, hairpin bends all the way down, we reached this most photographed prettiest beach on Lefkada, if not in the

Sappho's Leap (Akrotiri - southern tip of Lefkada)

One of the 3 beaches at Porto Katsiki
See cover for colour version

whole of Greece. It didn't even mislead by offering only shingle. At the bottom of the many steps we reached the three fine white sandy coves, backed by white cliffs and lapped by crystal clear turquoise sea. The middle beach had beds on, but they were easy to ignore as there were rocky outcrops between each cove. We bathed and rested a while - sheer bliss. Walking down the steps had not been too bad, but up was more work so we were in need of a cooling ice cream at the top and the 4 kantinas there all had reasonably priced snack food and drinks too. Again this was a day trip beach, rather than a resort, but well worth a visit.

We had to return mostly on the same road, but I think the roadworks we witnessed may have made an easier way through to Vassiliki the other side of this south pointing finger of Lefkada. At the high point after **Hortata** (Χορτάτα), we turned right to **Exanthia** (Εξάνθεια) built on the steep sides of a hill with many newer homes outside the centre. The roads were pretty good here although we were driving half way up a very steep sided valley with dramatic views. **Mount Stavrota** (Ορ. Σταυρωτά) and **Mount Elati** (Ορ. Ελάτη) dominate the centre top of the island but the area is quite fertile and green with many villages. We turned right at **Asprogerakata** (Ασπρογερακάτα) towards the mountain village of **Karia** (Καρυά).

Karia is a favourite inland stopping place for tourists with many rug and lace shops displaying their wares. It unexpectedly looked as if it may rain as we got out to explore. We took our black and white golf umbrella and were thankful we had when it did rain as we sat in the partially plane tree covered platia. The locals were amused by our umbrella sheltering us and our beers. We asked if there was somewhere to park for the night. They were surprised to hear we were English as most people they see with motorhomes

are German or Italian. Children played around the Grekovan in the car park as we cooked and ate our meal - a bit of a nuisance, but OK after a while. There were no other tourists there in the evening when we wandered round.

Next morning noisy building work started nearby at 7.30am - renovations on a lovely old style stone building, perhaps for offices rather than a house. We went back to one of the rug shops we'd looked in the previous day and bought 2 small rugs for our Lesvos house.

The road down to **Nidri** (Νυδρί), the main tourist resort and port on the island, was not all tarmac, but mostly good. At **Vafkeri** (Βαυκερή) we stopped for spring water. The church bell towers here were more dumpy than most other parts of Greece - square low buildings outside rectangular churches - perhaps more earthquake proof. The waterfall by **Rahi** (Ράχι) had been recommended, so parking up at the end of the road we walked alongside the river and aqueduct. After the tourist cafe there was a trickle of water alongside a narrow path, then rocks to a lower waterfall. We'd been warned 'the first one is not it ... keep going'. Up some wet steps and round two more corners we came to a very tall narrow waterfall, tumbling into a deep and cool pool (judging by the squeals of the Sunsail group as they climbed in for a swim). Yes it was quite spectacular. I couldn't get far enough away with my camera to get the top and the bottom in one photograph.

For a touristy resort I suppose **Nidri** is not bad. The parking was certainly well organised at the end of about 9 sideroads, with a board on the main road saying how many spaces in each. The long main road through the town was lined with shops, tavernas and bars. There was a harbour front with touristy tavernas with the dreaded 'greeters' trying to drag you in - no chance - and very varied prices. Lots of boats, no big hotels, not much beach and ferries from here to the nearby small and larger Ionian islands. We sampled the gyros pitta at a taverna in the main street. It was friendly, but they were amazed that anyone English tried to speak Greek. In the evening we found Roza's Ouzerie - a bright neon-lit place with sun-faded pictures of dishes on offer, but we'd been attracted by the word ouzerie. Roza was friendly, generous with 'tasters' and pleased to let us practise our Greek (I don't think she spoke much English) and the food was fresh and tasty, nothing like the pictures! When we had to return via Lefkada 2 weeks later and called in for a meal she greeted us like long lost regulars!

To the north was **Perigiali** (Περιγιάλι) but it seemed just a place to stay outside Nidri with not much more beach. **Nikiana** (Νικιάνα) a bit further on had an attractive working harbour, quite a few hotels and rooms and just a narrow shingle beach. It looked like a good spot for those who like 'messing about in boats'. We watched the house martins as they dived under the taverna canopy to their homes. At least 8 nests in a tiny area. The owner had put bits of cardboard boxes as a ledge under each to protect customers. The birds obviously thought they were convenient perches.

Opposite Nidri and to the south, the **Gheni** (Γένι) peninsular was mostly campsites and private homes with little seafront access. Southwest of here was **Poros** (Πόρος), a pretty mountain-side village and below, down a winding 4km road, is **Mikros Yialos** (Μικρός Γιαλός). Its pretty white pebble and shingle beach at the head of a bay is backed by those beautiful low branched trees with soft fernlike leaves and fluffy, fragrant red and yellow blossom (maybe a tree of heaven?). Behind are just a few tavernas, a well organised but expensive campsite and a few rooms.

We stopped the next night in rooms above a taverna on the sunny side of the next dogleg entrance horseshoe bay at **Sivota** (Σύβοτα) further round

Mikros Yialos beach

on the south coast - another 'yachties' resort. It was good to have a hot shower, wash some clothes and nibble a meze from the balcony overlooking the water and sailing boats as the sun went down.

We awoke early to the sound of cockerels. A peek outside revealed absolutely flat water, barely a ripple to be seen. Over breakfast on our balcony we looked out over masts and blue furled sails reflecting in the still water, the colours of the fishing boats spilling into the harbour water. Sea birds 'caw'ed, land birds 'tweet'ed. The chickens were more quiet now. There was just a murmur of Greek voices, the gentle sound of water splashing over paving as the taverna fronts were washed down. One sail boat gently glided out of the bay, the other sailors not in a rush to catch a whole day's sailing. A seagull, wings outstretched, barely moved as he glided round the bay - then suddenly swooped for a fish. A delivery van arrived, door flung open. Someone started banging in a new building opposite. The cockerels started to crow again and the day began.

Vassiliki

Vassiliki (Βασιλική) is the second busiest resort on Lefkada, frequented by windsurfer and watersports fanatics for its wide sheltered horseshoe bay. It has a reputation of attracting a young crowd. We didn't stay there overnight as we were getting the ferry to Kefalonia from here, but much preferred its laid back style, waterfront bars and tavernas and little narrow back streets to the plainess and tacky over-commercialisation of Nidri. The other side of the bay is a quieter spot at **Pondhi** (Πόνδη). It is not really a village, more an overspill resort at the other end of the bay, with more room for sunbathers and the watersports fans who can't all fit into Vassiliki.

We were impressed by Lefkada - its white beaches and turquoise seas, its variety of terrain, its Greekness inland and choice of resorts to suit all.

Lentils & Wild Flowers in Lefkada *by Mary Lambell*

Mary saw a different side of Lefkada on her walking holiday on this enchanting isle. Here we focus mostly on the parts of her article not covered in the previous report.

We'd enjoyed an autumn walking holiday in Pelion and Pindos, so decided to try another in Lefkada in May, followed by some relaxation. We found a week's guided walking based at **Agios Nikitas** (Αγ. Νικήτας) followed by a week in a villa about a mile up from the village, with car and swimming pool and with mountain and sea views - it sounded perfect.

Wild flowers by old stone building

Initially we were disappointed to be the only two booked on the walks due to some cancellations, but our leaders invited others to join so our group grew to ten. Ag. Nikitas only has about 8 families in the winter, but can get very busy in the height of summer. At the end of May it was pleasantly lively with a small beach ideal for our needs and fresh, locally caught fish in the tavernas.

Our first short walks took us around the village in different directions, one looking down on **Milos** (Μύλος) beach - beautiful, but inaccessible to the faint hearted except by boat. Some friends told us they had abseiled down on a rope attached to a rock above!

The next walk began at **Pigadisani** (Πηγαδησάνοι) and led across a vast fertile plateau filled with wild flowers in an abundance we had never experienced before. We passed a ruined monastery, **Agios Ioannis** (Αγ. Ιωάννης), far from any habitation and in the process of being restored. We ended our walk at **Karia**.

Another walk was from **Eglouvi** (Εγκλουβή) up an old mule path to the plateau where the lentils, for which Lefkada is famous, are grown. At the church of **Agios Donatos** (Αγ. Δονάτος) a festival is held at lentil harvest time and the

Ag. Donatos Church where lentil festival is held

lentils are cooked in large pots. There is a large open space with a number of wells still containing water. Dotted around the plain are stone buildings of varying sizes with domed roofs. Clearly they are old, but nobody seemed to know how old or what their function was - were they for housing farmers, donkeys or for storing the produce? Our guide book had no information and the date estimates of locals varied by several centuries.

We enjoyed a sunset walk from Ag. Nikitas to **Kathisma beach** (Παραλία Κάθισμα), another lovely stretch of white shingle where we swam then dined at the taverna there. While eating we watched dolphins out at sea and the walk back was illuminated by fireflies - quite magical.

Our final walk was from **Tsoukalades** (Τσουκαλάδες) down to the beach and around the coast to **Lefkas town** in the north. This is a very windy part of the coast, popular with windsurfers. The spit, known as **Gira** (Γύρα), is lined with windmills taking advantage of the prevailing winds too.

The guided walks week was helpful as an introduction to the island and to see areas we might not have otherwise explored. The villa was set amongst the olive trees and well equipped - but we did tear ourselves away to explore more of the island and even **Dodona** 3 hours away on the mainland in our second week. We came away aware that there were many more places yet to see and walks we'd like to do - in fact we returned to the same villa this year (2002).

How to get to Lefkada

By Air & Road - Nearest airport Preveza on mainland, then road via quick ferry across Amvrakikos Gulf and road bridge to Lefkada.

By Sea - ferries from Nidri & Vassiliki to Meganissis, Ithaki & Kefalonia

The Peloponnese in Autumn *by Carol and Denis Byrne*

Carol and Denis enjoy Autumn trips to the Peloponnese and here share some of their favourite places.

If it hadn't been for our friends Davis and Thalia owning a house on the Peloponnese, we would probably have never visited the area as, although we have been Grecophiles for many years, our focus had been on the islands.

The area is a land mass attached to mainland Greece through an isthmus into which the Corinth canal was carved finally in the 19th century, although many attempts were made over the centuries including those by Alexander the Great, Caligula and Nero.

Map adapted from Efstathiadis Road Atlas Summary

Remarkably it is an area which has been bypassed by mass tourism despite some of the loveliest scenery and beaches in Greece, or Europe in general. Granted there are areas which have become weekend retreats for Athenians and many tourists do visit some parts, especially Germans and Austrians, however there are many places which continue to have the appearance and 'feel' of the old Greece. Perhaps this is because some villages are quite remote, accessed only by difficult roads, or perhaps it seemed that way because we were visiting at a time when there are very few visitors. Whatever the reason October is a perfect time for enjoying the beauty of the countryside, the fascinating history of the area, and the pleasure of observing those aspects of the Greek way of life seemingly unchanged over the centuries.

It would be naïve to believe that life isn't changing here. With the influence of technology and membership of the EU; Lidl and Dia supermarkets are beginning to appear in larger towns where one can buy German and Spanish food and products, and the EU is funding numerous road improvements around the Peloponnese. However, walk out in the early morning and see the smoke rising from the delicious wood burning fires on the farms in the countryside, listen to the fishermen setting out before light to set their nets in the bays, watch the old and the young chatting away in village and town squares over the inevitable greek coffee. You can imagine that the same scenes have been repeated over hundreds of years.

There are places too numerous to mention in one article so I have concentrated on three areas which may not be so well known and which represent all that is special about this part of Greece and at this time of the year.

Take a trip behind the bay on which the lovely town of **Gythio** sits in the Laconian Gulf. Make your way to **Skala**, cross over the bridge across the **Evrotas** river and turn down a rough road at the side of the river, following this until it turns right or left behind the beach area. In taking this trip you will travel through the orange groves intensively farmed in the river valley and (sadly) drawing water from the river putting the water balance at risk. However, there are sea eagles, kingfishers and many other species of birds which feed and live in the area and provide a wonderful spectacle as you travel through. Leave the river and travel behind the beach area where hundreds of butterflies of many different species are busy feeding on the wild tarragon which is in flower and giving off a delightful scent in the warm sun. We took a motorbike but you can travel by car or foot. The butterflies flew round us and alongside us as if providing an escort as we slowly travelled along. Stop for a swim in the shallow waters of the bay whose beach stretches for miles, or take a walk around the dunes where a walkway and information boards have been set up to teach you about the flora and fauna of the area. Travel back up one of the many tracks which will take you through the farming villages in this delightful area.

Many people will have visited the ancient site at **Mystra** near to **Sparta** on the edges of the **Taygetos** mountains. The site and its environs provide an awe inspiring visit, lush greenery in the fertile river valley and the high moun-

Mystra (photograph by Sylvia Cook)

tains rising above the valley and into the distance, seemingly endless in number. We stayed on a campsite at the foot of the site of Mystra and within a stroll of the village of Mystras with its pleasant hotels and tavernas. The unexpected bonus occurred when we took a walk in the dark and to our delight found that the 13th Century fortress crowning the site high above us was floodlit, affording an amazing and very beautiful spectacle. Take the road from Sparta to **Kalamata** through the **Langada** pass to complete a breathtaking experience.

The third area to share with you focuses around the **Bay of Navarino** in Messinia province. We stayed on a campsite in the village of **Gialova** where there are also rooms and a small hotel. In ten steps we could walk out of our motorhome and into the sea. There were only eight campers or caravans on the site and we all had front line access to the sandy beach. Across the bay we could see the attractive town of **Pylos** and watch dramatic and beautiful sunsets behind the rocky headlands which form an almost complete land circle to the bay. There is much interesting history to this area with castles and museums to visit. The bay is surrounded by farmland. Of especial interest is a huge lagoon behind the bay, with a wonderful opportunity for birdwatching. These wetlands, and in fact the whole area, are protected and tourism is low key eco tourism. The air is so still that the smoke from the wood fires in the farms hangs in the air and gives a delicious autumnal scent; fig orange and pomegranate trees grow wild, offering their produce for you to pick and enjoy.

Only a sample, but some of our special experiences of this lovely part of the world.

Mykonos, Delos & Rinia Profile *by Sylvia Cook*

Delos (Δήλος) is the small sacred island *encircled* by the other Cycladic islands - hence the name of the island group. **Mykonos** (Μύκονος) to the east and **Rinia** (Ρήνεια) to the west are the nearest - the first developed and cosmopolitan, the other uninhabited and quiet. (See following pages.)

Mykonos was said to be the rock thrown by Poseidon to kill the giants during Zeus's Battle with the Giants, or the pile of

rocks heaped on top of them to make sure they did not return!

The island is mostly rocky and barren, 85 sq km surrounded by beaches, with **Mykonos Town** as its vibrant hub. The best sandy beaches have developed into resort villages. **Tourlos** (Τούρλος) and **Ag. Stefanos** (Αγ. Στεφάνος) to the north and the southwest beaches of **Ag. Ioannis** (Αγ. Ιωάννης), **Ornos** (Ορνός), **Plati Yialo** (Πλατύ Γιαλό) and **Paradise** (Π. Καλαμομόδι) are easily accessed from the town. Less crowded beaches can be found at **Elia** (Ελιά) and the beautiful spacious beach of **Kalo Livadi** (Καλό Λιβάδι) as their bus service is not so frequent - but it is best to visit outside high season if you are looking for the peace and quiet portrayed in the film 'Shirley Valentine'. The east coast is rugged and the north coast exposed to the Meltemi winds, but **Panormos Bay** (Ορμ. Πάνορμος) is slightly sheltered. In the north you just may find a quiet idyllic beach in a pretty bay accessed from a dirt road.

Whilst it is true that Mykonos is an expensive island, you can always find ways to manage on a modest budget and **Paradise Camping** is about the least expensive place to stay and is in a gorgeous setting.

Once THE place to be in ancient Greece, today **Delos** and the larger deserted island of **Rinia** are uninhabited and can only be visited on day trips.

Cycladic Sisters: Two Goddesses & A Temptress *by Aurelia*

The magic of Greece is in its very ambiguity, in the tensions that pull it from one wonderful, delicious extreme to the other. The senses are pleased and pampered by the serene beauty of Greece found in the depth of its vistas, the spectacular sunrises and sunsets, and the radiance of the light that even the poets cannot adequately describe. The senses are titillated and tempted, also, by Greece's extremes of food and drink, flesh, nightlife, music and the burning sun. These tensions intrigue and mystify the visitor - the barbarian who comes to the shores of Greece - but they are perfectly understandable to the Greeks who live every day with the conflicting realities of life in the land of the gods.

Perhaps this tension is best exemplified in the islands that form an ancient triangle in the very heart of the Cyclades. They are cosmopolitan Mykonos, sacred Delos, and mysterious Rinia. Taken together, these sisters with their distinctive and contradictory personalities give the visitor a tantalizing taste of a Greece known only to the Greeks.

Within this triangle, one can sunbathe nude or topless on some of the most beautiful beaches in Greece, literally dance until dawn at discos, take a magical, cruise through the islands, go back in time with the ancients on an island declared 'sacred' by the Greek government, or spend an enchanted day alone on an uninhabited island where gentle waves caress a pristine shore, luscious grapes hang from vines and where the pure air is so still you can hear yourself breath.

Mykonos' distinctive windmills - photo by Pauline Rowley

Mykonos - The sometimes naughty sister, Mykonos, is famous worldwide for its chalk-white beauty and its vibrant nightlife. Celebrities and dignitaries from all over the world make this island a destination to shop, sunbathe, party, and island hop, and cruise ships from all over the world come here. It is not unusual when walking through the whitewashed streets of the town centre, also called **Hora**, to see a famous model or movie star gazing into a jewellery store while munching on a cheese pie, looking very much like Audrey Hepburn in 'Breakfast at Tiffanys'. The glorious gold and jewel-studded rings, earrings, bracelets, and necklaces displayed in the windows of the artisans of Mykonos bedazzle even the most sophisticated celebrity.

Mykonos is pleasing to the senses. Its brightness will dazzle you and its pleasures enchant you. Mykonos, the temptress, will seduce you with her charms.

Delos - If Mykonos represents secular pleasures sought by the jet set, Delos is its opposite and is the most sacred of the Greek islands. At the geographical centre of the Cyclades, Delos is its spiritual centre too. It was the religious, cultural, and commercial capital of ancient Greece; a thriving commercial hub and the 'summer home' of the rich and famous of the time. One can see Delos' past glory in the magnificent ruins and in the exquisite, world-famous mosaic floors of the ruined palaces.

Rinia - The third sister is Rinia. A haunting, mysterious island four times the size of Delos and separated from it by a small strait. Called alternatively 'Great Delos' or 'Big Delos', it has two sections connected by a narrow isthmus - both parts uninhabited. By Greek law no one may live or build a permanent home there. It has no running water nor electricity and there are no roads on its rocky, hilly terrain. (There are rumours, however, of a few hearty souls who make the island their home). Very few tourists know about Rinia or think of going there, even on a day's excursion, so if you plan well, it is possible to be the only person on one of its four pristine, sandy beaches.

The Cycladic Sisters - Mykonos, Delos, and Rinia, each with her own personality, are among the most precious treasures of Greece. The visitor who ventures there will experience the sacred and the profane, the sublime and the absurd, the Ottoman and the Venetian, the glorious ideal and stark reality, the goddess and the temptress, the perfect beauty of the sun god, Apollo and the wild revelry of the wine god, Dionysos. In short, the visitor will experience Greece.

MYKONOS

Mykonos, one of thirty-three inhabited Cycladic islands forming an imaginary circle around Delos in the Aegean Sea, is considered by many to be the most cosmopolitan and sophisticated of the Greek islands. Mykonos offers the very best in accommodation, food and ambiance to the visitor. Perhaps nowhere else in Greece can one find gold jewellery as fine as that produced by the artisans of Mykonos. This reputation is due in part to the time when Venice ruled the island (12th-15th centuries) and the Venetian influence is seen today in the distinctive jewellery. Luxury yachts from all over the world dock at its harbours, ferries arrive daily from Piraeus and Rafina and more planes than ever before land on the island at the new airport built just a few years ago. Mykonos has more bars, restaurants, and discos than most other Greek islands and the quality of the beaches, food, music, precious jewellery and nightlife (if that is your scene) is second to none.

Alefkandra (Little Venice)

Many artists consider **Mykonos town** itself a work of art. Its white homes resemble sugar cubes and all the winding alleyways and joints between the paving stones are painted chalk white. The fishing harbour is small with brightly coloured caiques bobbing about in a sea so blue it looks like a postcard. If artists had been asked to design this town, they would have put domes with crosses on churches on a silhouette of cube-like homes and then added windmills for a picturesque contrast. But it was ordinary people who were the island's first artists, building the houses, churches and windmills using materials found on the island, allowing Mykonos to develop naturally. This approach to architecture has produced a town that is itself a work of art, a masterful collection of perfect, whitewashed cubes that stand in dazzling contrast to the brilliant, blue sea and sky.

The contrasts on Mykonos can best be seen early on a Sunday morning, between 6 and 8 am. Silently, worshippers returning to their homes share the streets with night people who have recently left the clubs and discos. Widows covered by traditional black dresses and head scarves pass young women scantily attired; each group stares in amazement at the other, saving their caustic comments for when they are safely out of earshot. Men and women selling produce from their donkeys stand far from young rent boys trying to make one more score before the 'night' ends. Music from nearby clubs plays softly, perhaps in deference to the hundreds of church bells tolling throughout the island.

Orthodox priests walk about in long, black robes that 'swish-swish' as they dust the cobblestones. Walking behind the priests, giggling uncontrollably, are tipsy drag queens with heavy make-up and orange-coloured hair, their long gowns 'swish-swishing' in unison with the priestly robes.

Shopkeepers open their establishments early on Sundays. Visitors can

Mykonos photo courtesy of Magical Journeys

peek into one of Mykonos' famous icon makers' studios. The walls are decorated with magnificent works of art in the Byzantine style, each an original, and beautiful icons of St. George and the Dragon and other saints on display. A few doors down the visitor comes upon a leather shop featuring expertly handmade leather handbags and sandals, side by side with harnesses, vests, gloves, and ominous-looking whips.

And then there is the sacred side of Mykonos. One of the architectural wonders on the island is **Paraportiani**, said to be the most photographed church in Greece. An architectural masterpiece, a complex of five churches built during the 16th and 17th centuries and perhaps earlier. There are about 500 churches on Mykonos, most of them small, private chapels attached to or near the homes of devout Mykonians. It is said that when the lives of the fishermen and other islanders were in danger while they were at sea, they would be spared if they vowed to build a chapel upon return to the safety of land, and that is why, the story goes, there are so many churches.

Mykonos town itself is a maze, deliberately built in this fashion to confuse pirates who came to rob and pillage. The maze makes the town more romantic and creates literal surprises around almost every corner.

In a typical home, a Mykonian woman sits beside her needlework or loom in a room sparsely furnished with simple yet artistic necessities. On the walls are icons and the floors are covered with hand-woven rugs. Outside, donkeys laden with baskets of produce are lead by Mykonians through the narrow, whitewashed pathways as motor bikes with attached carts zip rapidly through the lanes to deliver supplies.

Petros, the pink pelican and good luck symbol for the island, wanders about. He is seen most often in the **Alefkandra** section or in 'Taxi Square' near the harbour front where the statue of Mando Mavrogenous proudly stands. She is the famous heroine who gave all her fortune to support her country during the 1821 Greek War of Independence.

The town is made distinctive by its huge, round windmills, which once worked to grind wheat. Now they are the island's most famous symbol and their paddles share the skyline with the church domes and crosses, creating dramatic contrasts to the cube-like homes hugging the ground. The windmills are in beautiful Alefkandra, the loveliest corner of Mykonos.

Petros with Aurelia

Alefkandra has been painted and photographed by artists from all corners of the world and is called 'The Little Venice of Greece'. In this precious spot, rows of chalk white, square homes have turned their backs toward the sea, hunching their wooden terraces and brightly painted balconies over the creamy sea foam. Restaurants in Alefkandra become part of this incredibly romantic landscape by placing their tables as near as possible to the sea and covering them with tablecloths matching the brilliant red or blue colours of the balconies and terraces.

At sunset, the rosy fingered sky kisses the wine-dark sea, and the seduction is complete. The mortal savouring his glass of nectar in Alefkandra at sunset is favoured by the gods.

DELOS

According to mythology, Apollo, god of light and the sun, was born on Delos (also his sister Artemis, goddess of hunting). The island is drenched in sunlight. There are no high mountains or trees to provide shade. There is one palm tree, however, and it is said that this is where Apollo was born as his mother, Leto, leaned against the tree to give birth. Zeus chose Delos for the birth as a sanctuary for Leto, far from the eyes of his jealous wife, Hera. Delos means 'that which appeared' - so named because it suddenly appeared in the waves to shelter Leto from Hera's eyes.

Guidebooks and guides will tell you that no one is allowed, by law, to stay on Delos overnight, but there is a wonderful story about how Lawrence Durrell, the famous Philhellene and English author, managed to stay there. In his book, 'The Greek Islands', Durrell explains how he gained the cooperation of a boatman, and with a slight deception on the men guarding Delos, he spent a romantic and spiritual night on the sacred island under the protection of Apollo.

Durrell said the evening was perfect with Apollo protecting them, Zephyr controlling the calm breezes, and Aphrodite orchestrating the sunset. They swam nude by the rising moon and came back to drink warm soup and coffee from thermos flasks thoughtfully brought by Janko, the boatman.

As dusk fell, they snuggled in their sleeping bags, but were awakened at midnight by the brilliant, white light of the moon. Deciding to prowl among the ruins, they climbed over rocks and through barbed wire, and did not need lights because, according to Durrell, *"we could have read a newspaper by the moon's light."* They came upon what must have been the floor of an ancient villa and saw what looked like an ordinary fish design. Durrell went to the sea for a pail of water to splash over the floor, and, like a photograph developing in a tray, the head of the most beautiful dolphin emerged. It was one of the famous mosaics that would be viewed by the public in later years, but he and his wife saw it long before.

Delos Lions photograph courtesy of Magical Journeys

Durrell described Delos as *"silent and ominous"* at night with snakes and lizards slithering about, but he said it was also magical. When the moon gave up its brilliance, they slept once again and in the early morning the boatman returned and they returned to Mykonos.

The island itself is relatively small - six kilometres long and 1,500 meters wide - but is monumental in Greek history and mythology and was home to one of the most important and glorious civilizations the world has ever known.

In its day, there was no island in Greece as glorious as Delos - it was the ultimate destination point. It had an eclectic mix of mansions, temples, markets, stadia and shops, and one never knew who would suddenly turn up to visit or ask about establishing a summer residence. Rumour has it that Cleopatra wanted to build a summer home there, but the residents voted against it. Delos was the commercial, religious and cultural centre of ancient Greece, the jewel of the Aegean Sea - magnificent and majestic.

History tells us, that the island was probably first inhabited in 3000 BC and by the end of the 4th century BC it developed into a major commercial centre, competing with Rhodes. By Roman times, Delos had roughly 25,000 inhabitants. Archaeologists have uncovered evidence of Ionians living here in the 7th century BC, followed through the centuries by Athenians, Delians, Egyptians, Syrians, and Romans.

Delos' rule over the sea was established around 478 BC when a Delian confederacy was formed to bring neighbouring islands under its influence. Lavish festivals were held every five years to honour the gods; large barges brought animals from neighbouring islands for sacrifice, and the most nubile Delian maidens were chosen to dance and sing hymns in honour of the gods. It had been a burial ground for Delians, but some time around 426 BC, in order to secure the favour of Apollo (and incidentally, to gain control of the shrine's treasures), the bones of those who died there were removed to Rinia, where a new burial ground was created. From then on Delian women who were about to give birth and the elderly were taken to Rinia so that no one should be born or die on Delos.

The island's fall was sudden and brutal. In 88 BC during the Mithridatian War, all inhabitants were slaughtered and the mansions and temples desecrated and demolished. Next, the island was burned by an army of barbarians and for years after that pirates came to pick over the remains.

It was not until the late 19th century that archaeologists began excavations revealing the former glory of Delos and encouraged the Greek government to establish strict rules for the site. The French School of Archaeology began excavations in 1872 and in 1904 uncovered many public buildings and private houses - some they partly reconstructed. Work is still in progress. Five of the magnificent nine lions that are symbols of Delos have been removed to a museum to protect them from corrosion. The proud lions one sees now on the Avenue of the Lions are casts of the originals.

RINIA

Mighty pillars guard the entrance to the primitive paradise called Rinia, the third sister in this Cycladic triangle. On one side, the huge rocks are rugged and weather-beaten, their age hidden in the dark stones. On the other side, the surfaces are so smooth and shiny, reflecting rays of the sun, that the giant stones appear newly risen from a protective cave in Poseidon's bosom. Proud as sentries these pillars stand, ancient companions to the sea.

Tinted with deepening shades of blue, green and purple, the water is an artist's pallet. Near the shore, the colour is a subtle blue, becoming a bright blue/green and then a rich, dark, wine-coloured purple in its deepest part. Two lovely coves protect the deserted, sandy beaches.

Around 425 to 416 BC it became a burial ground for Delians (as above) and home to pregnant women and anyone about to die on Delos. One can see grave markers and burial stones on its rocky, hilly terrain. For centuries Rinia was a refuge for pirates. After the Greek War of Independence in 1821, it was ceded to its sister, Mykonos and is now part of the Cycladic Triangle. Now uninhabited, Mykonians bring their sheep and goats to graze and concrete huts are scattered about the island to provide temporary shelter in the event of storms.

Some tourists come here during the day to experience being almost alone on an uninhabited island, but very few. At times, night parties are held on the island and notices will appear in Mykonos announcing the event; all the available boats are chartered and revellers descend on the island with sleeping bags. They party all night, hoping the Meltemi winds will permit them to return the next day. These parties have been discouraged by officials in Mykonos because of obvious dangers.

Other Mykonians come to Rinia to fish and to escape the tourists. I was introduced to an elderly fisherman, Gregoris who took me there on three

occasions when he went to fish. He said he and his friends have had magical experiences there, coming together in a caique, bringing food and drink. They make a bonfire for cooking and for light, and they eat, drink, play bouzouki and dance under the brilliant, white moon. When night falls they sleep in the caique and, weather permitting, return to Mykonos the next day.

He dropped me off on one of the beaches, then went to his 'secret' fishing place. The first day I wore jeans and a long-sleeved shirt, carried my pen and notebook and studiously explored the island, looking for grave markers and other artefacts of burial sites. But on the next two occasions I wore my swimsuit under my jeans, took a picnic lunch and wine, practised yoga on the warm sand in my bathing suit, and swam natural in the crystal clear waters. All three times I saw no one else and was enveloped by a sense of peace and a stillness that is almost impossible to describe.

A friend who lives on Mykonos and is very familiar with Rinia went there with a companion in the early evening and described her extraordinary experience for me. *"We saw the sunset from high atop the most southern part of the island. If you looked to one side, the moon was out and full, with a still yet blue sky. If you looked the other way, the sun was setting. It was the most beautiful sight I have ever seen - a truly magnificent gift from the gods."*

The Cycladic Sisters - two goddesses and a temptress, three gifts from the gods. As you travel in this ancient triangle you will suddenly become enchanted and you will not know if it is because of Apollo, the sun god, Dionysos, the wine god, or Aphrodite herself, the goddess of love.

Aurelia is a freelance US writer and author of a novel "A Lone Red Apple" set on Mykonos, Delos and Rinia. See her website www.aloneredapple.com. In the UK her novel may be purchased from Hellenic Bookservice.

How to get to Mykonos, Delos & Rinia
By Air - Charter direct to Mykonos, Scheduled via Athens
By Sea - from Piraeus & Rafina to Mykonos, connections to many islands via Amorgos, Andros, Ikaria, Naxos, Paros, Samos, Syros, Tinos, etc. Local ferries & tours to Delos from Mykonos.

No Problem - Be Prepared *by Sylvia Cook*

Whether Island Hopping or going on a package holiday to an unknown destination, here are a few suggestions of useful things to take and tips for dealing with some frequently experienced niggles.

❑ Before you go - No need to take the whole guidebook to Greece, just photocopy the relevant pages for places you hope to visit. Even if you read them before, they are so much more relevant when you are there.

❑ Bring names and addresses for postcards written or printed on sticky labels. It takes the boring bit out of writing to friends and family and is much lighter than the whole address book.

❑ If moving around on holiday, pack your clothes in 2 or 3 rolls with a selection of beachwear, day time, evening and under-wear in each. Rolled clothes generally need less ironing and you can unwrap just one roll when you stop somewhere for just a night or two, leaving the others still packed for your next move.

❑ When travelling with someone else, swap one of your rolls for one of theirs in your case, holdall or backpack in case of problems. It is unlikely you would both lose your luggage on a flight or ferry crossing.

❑ I always take a few wire hangers as they are very light and so often there are not enough provided. If moving on you can roll up clothes still on the hangers, ready to go straight into the next wardrobe.

❑ Useful small extras to pack - a Swiss army style penknife and/or small vegetable knife. If you like to prepare your own simple breakfast, the occasional salad or a 'meze' for your evening drink, a sharp knife can be an invaluable and light addition to your packing, not always found in studio kitchens. Do pack it in your main case, NOT hand luggage - otherwise it may be confiscated at baggage checking.

❑ Studios include basic kitchen facilities, more than you are likely to use, but ask about making coffee if there are no cooking facilities in 'rooms'. Often they will provide a 'camping gaz' burner and small Greek saucepan for boiling water, or a shared kitchen area to make the occasional morning coffee or tea. Bring a small polythene bag of your favourite instant coffee or tea bags from home plus sugar and dried milk if you like it white - very light and convenient for repacking and cheaper than buying small jars and packs in Greece.

❑ Perhaps obvious, but don't forget a small alarm clock to get up for ferries in the early hours, and a torch for finding your room (or the keyhole) at night in off the beaten track places.

❏ It is thankfully becoming quite common to have a refrigerator in simple rooms, but unless it is designated a 'studio' you may not have glasses (or decent sized glasses) supplied. If there are none you are sure to find some quite cheaply in the supermarket and you can bequeath them to the last room when you leave. The morning fruit juice, evening wine or beer and even water does taste better out of a glass.

❏ Always have a few tissues or a pieces of toilet roll in your pocket or handbag - it saves embarrassment when the taverna loo has run out.

❏ If your wash basin has no plug, make a temporary one by cutting a circle slightly larger than the plug hole from a washing up cloth (from the supermarket). Put a suitably sized bottle top or pebble over it to help stop the water going down. Unless the fit is very good it will still drain away, but very slowly. Better still, take a universal size plug (with wide lip) with you as this is a common problem.

❏ If you are an avid reader on holiday, try to get second hand paperbacks or books you don't mind leaving behind once you've read them - or exchange them for others if you find an enterprising tour office or bar with an exchange scheme (often run by ex-pats who want something to read themselves).

❏ And from Janet Ellis for those who like walking off the beaten track - Take a piece of chalk in remote areas. Mark tree trunks or large stones as you go if you think you may need to retrace your steps!

Let us know if you have any tips for travelling in Greece, or tell us what your 'little luxury' is that you can't be without, or your 'Words of Wisdom' - those little things that experience on Greek holidays has taught you.

Island Hopping

We have over 22 years years experience of organising island hopping holidays within the beautiful Greek Islands. With a choice of over 57 islands and 11 mainland destinations to choose from, you can either select one of our set routes or tailor make your own itinerary - calling on our knowledge and considerable experience to assist you. Why not contact us on:

Telephone: **01580 860733** or

email: **enquiries@islandwandering.com**

First Experiences, The Changing Face of Corfu *by Dave Rodda*

The impressions formed on his first trip to Greece in 1971 led to a lasting love affair for Dave Rodda. In spite of the inevitable changing face of the places he first visited, just a mention of one of those resorts in Greek-o-File was enough to bring the memories flooding back and compel him to write to us.

My first visit to Greece was in 1971 when I travelled with a friend from college by train as far as Brindisi, via a change in Milan (an experience in itself). We arrived on Corfu on the ferry from Brindisi at around 8am. On clearing customs we noticed a cafe 'Dirty Dicks' and went there for breakfast. Having eventually sorted out the bus timetable, we caught a bus to **Dassia** where we pitched our tent at the campsite.

Soon after arriving a leaky water tanker pulled up by the campsite and an old lady rushed out of her small house to take advantage of this abundance of fresh water.

The evening took us across the road to a taverna where we were introduced to the Greek custom of choosing your meal from the dishes simmering away in the kitchen. After a delicious meal and plenty of cheap wine we made our way back to the campsite to find some late arrivals putting up their tent by the light of their car headlights. It was not long before things settled down and everyone went to sleep. However, we were woken early next morning by a commotion from our neighbouring tent. On investigation we found out that in the dark they had inadvertently pitched their tents over an ants' nest - and the ants were making their complaints known.

From Dassia we moved on to **Paleokastritsa** where we stayed for the next two weeks. At one point on the bus journey there the conductor left the bus to visit a roadside shrine and the impatient driver decided to continue, the conductor running after the bus was quite a spectacle.

Paleokastritsa 1971

We soon became friendly with the Paleokastritsa campsite owner who liked to practise his English on us. Once he took us to his home village where he introduced us to the delights of fresh figs.

At this time of year the roads became very smooth and slippery. The authorities' solution seemed to be to spray the road with wet tar - I don't know what the motorists thought of this, but as pedestrians we were not impressed. Our route to the beach took us past the Paleokastritsa hotel and their grotto, then down through the village. Owing to the wet tar on the roads we started taking a path along the headland which eventually led down to the beach. Sadly on a return visit in 1977 (with my wife) we found this route blocked by a large hotel (Akrotiri Beach Hotel I think) now occupying the headland.

By crossing the road from the campsite following various paths, one a dried up river bed, and finally scrambling down a small cliff, you arrived at a deserted beach where the only sign of habitation was an old hut. Behind the beach was a dirt track which led up to the village of **Liapades** and then onto a road leading back to the campsite. Now this deserted beach is a resort in its own right.

Liapades 1977

We decided after a while that it was time to see some of the sights of Greece and left Corfu to visit Delphi and Athens (another story!) On the evening before we left Corfu we met an American Greek over on his annual leave. He told us he owned some land in Kassiopi where one day he hoped to build a hotel. He invited us to camp there on our return and we arranged to meet him in the same taverna in **Corfu Town**. We duly met up with him and travelled together on the morning caique to **Kassiopi**.

Once there we were taken out of the village along the coast road to a pebble beach where the owner proceeded to chase his neighbour's chickens from his land, yelling abuse at his neighbour at the same time. He returned to Corfu Town. Despite the beauty of the area, a couple of nights sleeping on pebbles convinced us to return to Paleokastritsa for the remainder of our holiday.

By 1977 Kassiopi had started to wake up to tourism, but was still essentially the same small village. However, by the time I stayed there with the my family in 1994 the village had grown enormously to its present day sprawl. It would have been nice if the American Greek's hotel was built, but on investigation we found only a run-down block of apartments and the beautiful beach largely destroyed.

Another early memory of Corfu is taking our children abroad for the first time to **Benitses** Easter 1984. At this time the sand for the beach was still piled up in the village square, ready to dump on top of its natural pebbly beach.

Fortunately the northeast of Corfu still has places worth visiting, such as Lawrence Durrell's **Kalami** and its neighbouring village of **Kouloura**, also the undeveloped beaches of **Avlaki** and **Goyevinas** which are easily reached on foot from Kassiopi. We understood this area was owned by the forces so off limits in 1971, but this was no longer the case in 1994. Another favourite along this stretch is the picturesque village of **San Stephanos**.

It was during that first Greek holiday in 1971 that I was given a useful piece of advice. A Frenchman we met told us that wherever he went he looked for where Club Med were and got as far away as possible. Now following this philosophy, whatever the island, I look for where the major tour operators go and choose a different resort.

Whilst I have now visited many Greek islands and have not been back to Corfu since 1994, it still retains its place as one of my favourites because of its natural beauty and the memories it holds for me.

Also, and probably most importantly, it introduced me to the magic of Greece.

* * *

It seems that Corfu was the first Greek island for many - but everyone notices the changes. Here is a snippet from a letter from **Carol Kelly** *:*

I first fell in love with Greece in 1976 when I went to a very quiet resort on Corfu (Benitses). There were 2 hotels, a few villas with private beaches and a handful of tavernas. Corfu was very pretty then, hardly any development to speak of and I still recall the time we were in the hills behind the beach, perfectly still and quiet, when an elderly Greek man appeared as if from nowhere to offer us almonds.

I've seen pictures of Benitses since then and I've never been back! But I'm sure there are still some beautiful places on Corfu, which are not over-developed.

Ikaria Profile *by Sylvia Cook*

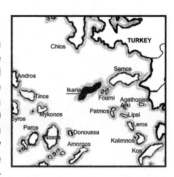

West of Samos, east of Mykonos and south of Chios, the island of **Ikaria** (Ικαρία), in the East Aegean group, is just 40km end to end and a maximum of 9km across. The **Atheras** (Αθέρας) mountain range forms a high barren backbone rising to over 1000 metres. The south slopes steeply with rocky terrain, and the north more gently through oak, pine and olive trees to the mostly unsheltered coast. Most of the villages are on the northern side, set in steep sided valleys fed by a good water supply. Farming and fishing are the main occupations here.

Armenistis (Αρμενιστής) in the northwest is the most commercialised resort on the island due to its nearby beaches, but it is certainly not targeted at the 'mass' market. **Evdilos** (Εύδηλος) is a pretty uncommercialised fishing village on the north coast where Samos ferries stop. On the south east coast, near the island's administrative centre and main port of **Agios Kirikos** (Αγ. Κήρυκος), many, mostly elderly, Greeks flock to **Therma** (Θέρμα) for the therapeutic hot springs. At one time there was a sign welcoming you to 'Ikaria - the island of radiation' since replaced with a less controversial welcome. As with many islands, Ikaria has a unique character and charm.

Ikaria Background

❑ *Ikarus escaped from Crete with his father, the inventor Daidalos, using feather wings stuck on with wax - but Ikarus was enjoying the experience and flew too close to the sun. The wax melted and he plunged to his death near the island, shaped like a wing, that now bears his name.*

❑ *The island was inhabited from stone age times, then by the early Greek Pelasgians and Carians. By the 8th century BC the Ionians settled from Miletus, but the Persians enslaved them in 512 BC. The following years, it followed a similar course to other nearby islands.*

❑ *In Byzantine times Ikaria was a place of exile for generals and other officials who didn't fit in with the current politics. The Franks then Genoese ruled before the island fell to the Turks in 1521, but in July 1912 the Ikarians rebelled and were briefly an independent state, even minting their own coins. By October 1912 they reunited with Greece.*

❑ *Ikaria has a reputation as a rebellious left-wing political stronghold, perhaps because 'Communist' dissidents were again exiled there (15,000 amongst 7,000 locals) in the late 1960s. Neglected by Athens, the islanders seem less fashionable and more self reliant to this day.*

Ikaria - An Island Apart
by Sylvia Cook

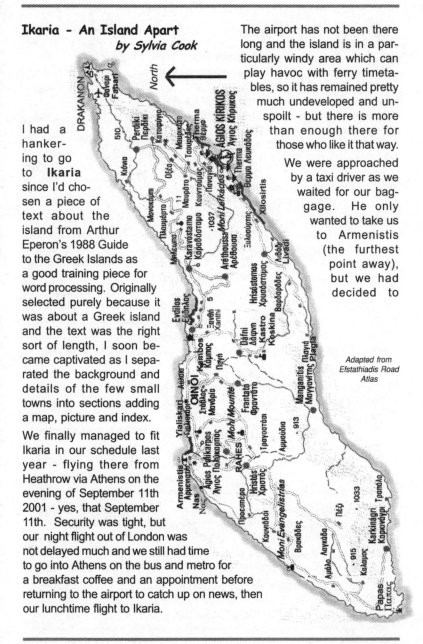

Adapted from
Efstathiadis Road
Atlas

I had a hankering to go to **Ikaria** since I'd chosen a piece of text about the island from Arthur Eperon's 1988 Guide to the Greek Islands as a good training piece for word processing. Originally selected purely because it was about a Greek island and the text was the right sort of length, I soon became captivated as I separated the background and details of the few small towns into sections adding a map, picture and index.

We finally managed to fit Ikaria in our schedule last year - flying there from Heathrow via Athens on the evening of September 11th 2001 - yes, that September 11th. Security was tight, but our night flight out of London was not delayed much and we still had time to go into Athens on the bus and metro for a breakfast coffee and an appointment before returning to the airport to catch up on news, then our lunchtime flight to Ikaria.

The airport has not been there long and the island is in a particularly windy area which can play havoc with ferry timetables, so it has remained pretty much undeveloped and unspoilt - but there is more than enough there for those who like it that way.

We were approached by a taxi driver as we waited for our baggage. He only wanted to take us to Armenistis (the furthest point away), but we had decided to start our visit this side of the island. We found another taxi and went to **Therma** (Θέρμα) - he said **Fanari** (Φανάρι) and **Kerama** on our map were just beaches - with no rooms to rent.

Therma looked just perfect for us as we approached from above. The taxi driver stopped by Rena's rooms, which he obviously knew, but we thought we'd relax with a beer at the sea front first and then look around - thinking we would have plenty of choice. Service was slow, but that suited us fine.

When we were ready we thought we'd try the rooms the driver had recommended, but there was no-one there mid afternoon. We tried a few other places nearby - all full. It seems that September is THE season for the elderly Greeks who are the majority of visitors here. We went back to the Rena and after speaking to some guests who thought there was a room free, we waited, sat outside for over an hour until Rena returned - but there was no room at the inn! She suggested a couple of places nearby. They had rooms but no private facilities. Terry left me with the bags and searched further afield, finding a very tiny room available at Agriolykos Pension on top of the cliff, accessed by walking through a derelict hotel. The room at least had a small bathroom and a chance to move into a bigger room the next day, so we went there. It had bright blue shutters, white walls and gorgeous views from several shaded or sunny seating areas looking across the bay or over the sea to Fourni and to Samos. The less attractive elements of dilapidated hotels could not be seen from here. It was that wonderful mix of simplicity, eccentricity, serenity and beauty that we have come to love.

Therma is very different from anywhere we've been before. There was nothing there to attract young people, but there were several tavernas and

Therma

kafeneions full of elderly Greeks and just a few other tourists, a few shops, supermarkets, tour offices, two kiosks and two very busy telephones. The hotels and guest houses were mostly older, functional and small. All day and evening there were people wandering about Therma in bath robes, their heads wrapped in towels, coming from the old fashioned spa baths building with 'ΥΔΡΟΘΕΡΑΠΕΥΤΗΡΙΟ' written above the entrance (Hydrotherapio Clinic), or the natural sauna in a cave at the end of the harbour. The more able elderly were standing around, chest to shoulder height in the sea in their swimming costumes, chatting and enjoying the warm September water. Although a few visitors were clearly unwell and hoping for miracles, most seemed to be enjoying themselves. It put me in mind of that science fiction film where alien 'pods' are dumped in a swimming pool near an old folks home, the old folk sneak in for a swim and are rejuvenated. Apparently some Greeks go to Therma 'on prescription' to take the natural radioactive waters, diverted from natural springs and piped through the baths.

We enjoyed a light taverna meal the first night, but the next night started with an ouzo meze (big meze) at a harbourside ouzerie, then after a stroll went to the end taverna which served souvlaki pitta. It was packed full of older Greeks. One man took out his harmonica and played hauntingly - we ordered a second small carafe of wine to stay and listen, recognising quite

a few of the traditional Greek tunes he played.

We were told there is another hot spring nearby, so we walked round from the narrow path leading from our pension, above the cliffs and down to the rock pool to investigate. It was surrounded by colourful striped layered rock. The water was deep and with difficult access, so not being much of a swimmer I sat on the edge, dangling a foot in the pool. I could clearly detect hot and cool currents.

We caught the bus from Therma to nearby **Aghios Kirikos** (Άγιος Κήρυκος) Friday morning, and were held up by the crowds outside a church where the priest was distributing bread from large baskets. It was 14th September so must have been the 'Exaltation of the Cross' *Ipsosi tou Stavrou,* the last major summer festival of the Greek Orthodox church. The bus wound up the valley and down the next.

Ag. Kirikos is today's administrative centre and main town of the island. Most of the ferries

Backstreet taverna, Ag. Kirikos

arrive here. Towering above the long white harbour wall which proclaims a welcome to the island of Ikarus is a modern metal monument to the mythological island namesake who flew too close to the sun. There is no beach here and few non Greek tourists, but there was a pleasant feel to the small town ramshackle streets and the tamarisk shaded cafe tables by the road, unfortunately overlooking a parking area in front of the harbour. We checked out bus details for our journey to the north of the island next day before returning to Therma.

With no transport, we didn't make it to **Therma Lefkados** (Θερμά Λευκάδος) further west which also has hot springs in a rock lined pool and a beach between rocky outcrops, nor to the shingle beach and scattered village of **Xilosyrtis** (Ξυλοσύρτης) also in the south.

Our Therma rooms had not been the best value, perhaps because of the shortage, but food and drink prices were very reasonable this side of the island. The Greek tourists were friendly and the atmosphere relaxed. It was not a late night place and we retired early to our rooms, sitting outside for a nightcap and talking to an English couple a few times. Our last night we were talking quietly (I swear), but a young American came out and asked us to be quiet - it was late,10pm, and he was there for the treatment!

There had been some confusion about a Saturday bus to the north of the island, now that it was mid September, but a local tour office checked for us and confirmed it would run to Evdilos next day. The sea was calm, so we took the ferry caique to Ag. Kirikos this time - much quicker than the bus. Terry stayed with the bags whilst I wandered with my camera, then we had a coffee to kill a little more time, before double checking the bus time at the tour office we'd been to yesterday. This time a different person was there who said there was no bus on Saturday! We asked others and got the same reply. Ah well, it would have to be a taxi. It took us ages to find one, but the pretty young lady taxi driver who eventually came by was the best taxi driver we've ever had in Greece.

Her taxi was an old, well cared for Toyota and she drove it slowly and sedately as the road wound higher and higher up the steep slopes, round hairpin bends, with spectacular views down to the coast and out to Fourni

Evdilos - Alpha Bank with our rooms above in centre

and Samos. It was very green on the high ridge that separates the north of the island from the south. There had been a cloud sitting on that ridge most of the time we had been on Ikaria, so it should not have been surprising. What was odd was that we didn't see any sheep or goats, mostly green shrubs, then more trees as we descended the other side, then the land was more dried out as we got closer to the north coast. The road snakes up and down around the valleys on sharp hairpin bends, through several small villages until from the next valley you see **Evdilos** (Εύδηλος) the houses nestling prettily on hill slopes and around the bays and harbour. It was once the capital of the island and is still a regular stop off for some ferries.

After our problems getting a room at Therma, we decided to go straight to one we'd been told about by an American Greek lady who had shared our taxi from the airport. She said she had rooms above the new Alpha Bank by the harbour so we headed straight there. She had one room available but just needed to get it cleaned for us - so we went for a wander and a spot of lunch. Evdilos is a proper small Greek town with little tourism, probably just a few independent travellers. We saw no signs of package tourism.

It has a wide square bay with some cafes around, a few houses, 2-3 tavernas and supermarkets at the head of the bay. The small sandy beach was not really big enough for sunbathing and rather public, but probably good for a quick swim. Round the headland (past the Alpha Bank) was a parking area which seemed to be cleared in readiness for a new harbour and just beyond was a shingle beach with very few people on it - perfect for a few last rays before the sun went down behind the rock. Our room being the last available was once again very small and had yet another sink with no plug - where do they all go? We had a narrow balcony at the front which we could just about sit out on, and a superb view of the bay and opposite hillside whilst we sipped an early evening beer and meze from the supermarket.

Ann and Spiros who owned our rooms had also run a taverna below the previous year, before selling it to the bank - a useful addition to the town. They still had a small bar area, but were busy renovating, expecting to reopen just the bar for drinks, mezes and loukoumadia in 2002.

The next day as we explored we realised the town was a little bigger than we had at first thought, but shops and a few bars on the upper slopes had closed now the August Greek tourist rush was over.

We hired a car that evening and set off towards the inland village of **Xristos Rahes** (Χριστός Ράχες) or

Xristos Rahon, where we heard they live a night time life with shops only opening in the late evening, and even schools teaching children in the afternoon or evening. We drove inland through an area devastated by forest fires a few years ago. There were many local traditionally built low stone houses in the area, built and roofed with thin rock slates - I don't know if many are lived in today, but most appeared to be in reasonable condition. Higher inland was fertile farmland surrounding the village of Xristos and its satellite hamlets which make the 'rahes' (meaning ridges) region. Apart from the fire damaged parts it is ideal walking country, but you would really need a car to continue down to the south coast to the little visited **Karkinagri** (Καρκινάγρι).

We reached Xristos Rahes too early, before 8pm. The centre of the town is paved, car free and was hushed. One taverna was open playing good Greek music. Opening time here is 10pm to 4am for most shops, although the bakery and one supermarket were just opening as we left. The people in this area are still resisting attempts to make them conform. This was the main area the 'exiled' socialists and communists settled not so long ago. Some places may open around lunchtime - but don't expect to find anyone up in the morning.

We went down to **Armenistis** (Αρμενιστής) for our evening meal finding a different route down an unfinished but reasonably flat road and came out close to the resort. It is a pretty resort, sitting on a rocky outcrop on the northwest corner of Ikaria overlooking the long beaches of Livadhi and Mesakti to the east, but clearly different from the rest of the island in that its hotels, bars and tavernas are geared towards package tourists - albeit of the more discerning kind. It was also more expensive than the rest of the island, but we enjoyed our meal at Charley's. He was friendly towards all and appreciated our attempts at speaking Greek although he spoke fluent English.

Next day we had hoped to breakfast at **Kampos** (Κάμπος), near the ancient capital of *Oinoi*, but there seemed nowhere open - perhaps the Rahi region's nocturnal habits suit other villages too. We drove inland again to look around. There was heavy cloud above us, but spectacular views down to the sunny coast which we returned to, stopping near the picturesque harbour of **Gialiskari** (Γιαλισκάρι). Here a blue domed church juts out into the sea, forming a picture postcard backdrop to the wide sandy beaches be-

Gialiskari church & fishing boats

tween it and Armenistis. It's a small fishing village with a few tavernas, some only open in the evening, but we found one for a coffee before exploring the fishing boats and church, then moving on.

The wide sandy beaches east of Armenistis are one of the few places in Greece good for surfing and were once frequented by hippies. With opposition from the authorities they have mostly moved away, or to the area around the only nudist beach, at **Nas** (Νας) to the west of Armenistis. Three or four tavernas and some accommodation for rent sit at the top of a steep gorge overlooking the small cove of Nas and the river ending in a lake as it

doesn't make it to the sea in the summer. The foundations of a 5th century BC temple to Artemis are here too and the tavernas are a welcome spot to relax before and after the many steps down to the enclosed sand and shingle beach - the shelter was appreciated as it was very windy this end of the island. The cloud was still over the mountains but we were in sun.

It was Aghia Sofia's day and there was feasting at a taverna outside Kambos on our way back. We had heard they enjoyed a good feast day on this island - also that the local wine is particularly good. We drove back through

Evdilos to have a quick look at **Karavostamo** (Καραβόσταμο) a little further east. It seemed a pleasant sleepy village with a one way system which sent us through trees on a dirt track down to the sea - but the locals were ignoring the traffic directions now the summer season was over. We had one last night in Evdilos and a lazy day before catching the Dolphin hydrofoil the next afternoon to Samos.

We had enjoyed Ikaria. It was a quiet relaxing island, but with plenty to see and do. Mid September it was closing down, the only exceptions being the elderly Greeks taking the waters in Therma and the English packaged tourists still filling the Armenistis tavernas. We had found the locals friendly, although guide books had warned otherwise and we liked the prices in most places too. As our hydrofoil passed by **Cape Drakanon** (Ακ. Δρακανον) on the eastern tip of Ikaria we saw the round white Hellenistic tower, dating from Alexander's time, and were pleased we had finally visited this very different Greek island.

Hydrofoil arriving at Evdilos

How to get to Ikaria

By Air - via Athens, then Olympic Airways to Ikaria, or charter to Samos then ferry. No direct charter flights.

By Sea - daily ferries Piraeus to Ag. Kirikos (can switch to Evdilos depending on weather), well connected via links with Chios, Fourni, Mykonos, Samos. Hydrofoil to/from Evdilos for Chios & Samos.

First of the Summer Retsina *by Arthur Deeks*

Subscribers to the Greek-o-File quarterlies, will remember Arthur Deeks' antics on holiday in Greece with travelling companion Harry in his 'Last of the Summer Retsina' and subsequent 'When Harry Met ...' articles. This prequel, subtitled 'Life before Harry' will entertain whether or not you read his later experiences.

Walking and visiting archaeological sites are my standard justification for taking lots of holidays in Greece, but the reality is that eating and drinking alfresco has got to be a major reason. Not for us self catering (shudder) or even sipping the duty free on the balcony, no it's the kafeneion, ouzerie, taverna, zakharoplastio. These have always been a primary source of enjoyment to us, whether eating, drinking, playing scrabble, reading, people watching, finding mis-spellings on the menu or on signs nearby. Apart from sleeping we only stay in accommodation to eat in the mornings.

I know it's cheap to laugh at other nations' abuse of English, when as a nation we are so pathetic at learning other languages, but I do find the errors amusing and collectable. I have a charming leaflet about a trip on the Elli Express from Lefkas *'and in the afternoon a very dos e passing around - giving good informations ... have a nice holidays'* (sic). I particularly liked the sign that used to be over a taverna near Lake Voulismeni in Agios Nikolaos, Crete - *'95% of the cast of The Lotus Eaters ate here'.* I often wondered what happened to the other 5% - did they bring sandwiches?

Nothing to do with tavernas but there used to be a sign on the beach on Patmos *'On the holy island of Patmos ... nuding is not aloud'* . I always assumed therefore that you could nude quietly if you wanted to.

Mind you all tavernas are nice or interesting or bizarre or a context for weird happenings.

Once on a Sunday on Samos with my wife, after an exhausting and appetite building cycle ride up in some hills, we were desperately hungry and happened upon a village which appeared to have no tavernas. Then we saw an old ice cream cabinet on a veranda and a couple of blue chairs and we thought - *Yes!* It was all a bit sparse but inside was a family already eating so we sat down at the remaining table. A man got up from the family and came across and (as I had even less Greek then than now) I managed by sign language to suggest that we would like to eat and drink. He returned to the 'family' table, emptied two of the glasses on the floor, filled a jug from the barrel and dished out two plates of something from a pan on the stove. It dawned on us, this wasn't a taverna at all but a private house. We ate up silently, offered money (refused, but we left it anyway) and fled down the hill. Moral: don't leave your freezer outside your house or you may get uninvited visitors.

Even more bizarre was an encounter which began in a self service taverna next to the Ag. Anagyri beach on Spetses, where my wife and I met an ample Greek lady with a spectacular appetite. A forceful personality matched her size and we were quickly drawn into conversation. Subsequently we had her life story in instalments, in the taverna, by the beach, on the beach, on the boat from the beach (the one that always played Vivaldi on the sound system) - there was no escape. She insisted we met her for a meal that evening. The taverna up the hill behind the old harbour was roadside. She was waiting for us with a variety of relatives, friends and her boyfriend, a hefty weather-beaten, builder from Athens with great callused hands and a guitar. Tables were imperiously ordered to be pushed together and resited actually **in** the road, but the passing light traffic was only occasionally inconvenienced. When we were all seated, she ordered the meal or rather a variety of meals, which, when served she (who must be obeyed) sent back. *"Yiannis will play some folk songs while we wait."* Yiannis began to sing loudly, and very flat. A sad song about I know not what. Suddenly, p*lunk!* a string went. A moment's pause and he carried on with the remaining five, even more discordant than before. The food was re-served, we ate, talked, and Yiannis continued playing. *Plunk!* another string went. He carried on. More food went back and more was ordered. *Plunk!* yet another string. Finally Yiannis gave up. A young relative leaned across to me and asked if I liked Greek folk music. *"Oh yes"* I lied, *"I will send you a record but, um, could you do something for me?"* , *"Of course"* , *"Send me an English body building magazine"*, *"Er certainly"*, *"Um - a women's body building magazine"* , *"Er, r-i-g-h-t"* (I didn't find one in my branch of W.H.Smiths, and I was too embarrassed to ask, so I sent him one for men.)

The evening didn't end there, it got worse. *"You must hear some real Greek folk music. We go to a club"* and she led us down to the harbour where she began endlessly negotiating with separate horse drawn taxi carriage drivers for an impossibly large and slightly inebriated group. We were in and out of carriages like a Whitehall farce as the drivers found alternative and more coherently organised employment. Eventually she managed to persuade three carriages to stand still long enough for the whole party to embark and there followed a visit to the alleged folk club, which, when we got inside, turned out to be a night club of extraordinary gloom and of the head banging variety. In the dark and utterly exhausted we managed to slip away, walked home and hid for the rest of the holiday. Some months later I received a record in the post - it was Greek heavy metal.

I have never shared Hugh Johnson's (that doyen of wine correspondents) view of Retsina that 'it tastes of turpentine and only serves to take away the awful taste of Greek food'. I know a lot of people who turn up their noses at Retsina and I will concede it's an acquired taste, but one that can be hastened by a chastening experience. In my pre-retsina days I went on an organised walking holiday to Ithaki and Kefalonia with a group of people who were mainly as 'mature' as I am now but also apparently abstemious.

We dined together in simple tavernas where the very reasonable price had been negotiated by the leader. On the first night when the waiter offered drinks they unanimously declined. I ordered my bottle of Demestica, but when it arrived, overcome by guilt, I offered the company a glass (safe in the knowledge that they didn't want a drink). Wrong! Collectively their glasses were raised, *"How kind"* and I was left contemplating my, by now, almost empty bottle. Second night - although I offered more quietly - was a repeat performance. Third night the small down-market back street taverna only had Retsina. I offered it half heartedly to the group who unanimously frowned, pouted and declined. And that, dearly beloved, is how, after two weeks I grew to love Retsina. (No actually they were a grand bunch - honestly.)

Kafeneia are another rich source of variety and interest, particularly when taking the pre-prandial (and strictly medicinal) ouzo. One challenge for Harry (my usual travelling companion) and I, is to find the kafeneion which serves the largest and most succulent free mezes. We have come across some wonderfully interesting ones, not always in the most salubrious surroundings. In fact one of our favourites to date is a scruffy caravan parked by the jetty in Tolon. We are still seeking the Holy Grail - the one that gives you so many mezes that you're too full to go to the taverna for a meal.

Of course Greek hospitality is legendary but it took me a couple of early experiences to work this out. The first time I was staying in a small village outside Rethymnon. The rep at the airport, as she handed over the keys to my car, warned me to make my mind up either to ignore my neighbours or suffer the consequences.

"What consequences?", "You'll find out" she said enigmatically.

The accommodation was one of a terrace of small, simple, single storey cottages with a tiny veranda separated from the next by a waist high wall. When I arrived I had noticed a middle aged lady tending her allotment. Later, as I sat out on my veranda relaxing after the journey, a voice from next door said *"You like?"* and there on the wall was a plate of what I would then have described as 'nibbles'. No person, just a voice and the plate. I remembered the rep's warning, but thought what harm could it possibly do. I ate them, replaced the plate, shouted *"thanks"* in English and sank back in my chair.

"You like?", "Very nice thank you" and there she was; the lady from the allotment with a big smile and another plate. I rushed inside for my phrase book, but she was gone and I had to eat it. What the hell it would be rude to refuse. After a couple more plates I finally managed to insist that I really would be ill if I ate anymore. The grim reality of the rep's warning began to sink in. I couldn't sit out without being fed and took to hiding if I thought she was about. In the end her small son confided (in perfect English) that it would be easier for his mother if I just ate with the family. So in the end I did, invariably with an audience of locals standing round the walls.

"This is our friend from England", "Ah, yassas."

A young lady who once worked for me and who'd had a 'difficult' marriage to a Greek, told me that I had been 'bought'. I prefer to think it was philoxenia at work and anyway on that basis I'm up for sale any day!

On the same holiday up in the mountains I stopped for a midday beer at a small kafenion, and the three old chaps engrossed in their game of tavli, barely raised their eyes. The proprietor gave me my beer. He was a dead ringer for the bar owner in the TV ad for Stella Artois, you know the one *"Fut desole"*. I mimed food and he shrugged meaningfully, but fortunately the three old guys sprang to their feet and left to return minutes later with eggs, bread, etc., which the proprietor cooked over a small primus type stove.

Much as I love England, I do miss Greece when I'm not there and to remind

me of it I have tried to recreate a piece of Greece in a corner of my garden. I have a fig, lemon, small olive tree, grape vine and eucalyptus tree - though I really need some of those large olive oil cans in which they grow geraniums or basil in Greece. OK so my oleander popped its clogs, the lemon tree spent all winter shedding leaves in my study and the one lemon clings tenuously to a branch. My grapes are minuscule with disproportionately large seeds, my olive tree only had one tiny olive, <u>but</u> it's a fig a day in the summer - providing the wasps don't get them first.

Harry is very sarcastic about my efforts, *"When's the wine festival this year, ho, ho, ho?"* and *"Is that an extra virgin olive?"*. But then I suppose he can be excused as he was a Rural Science teacher in one of his many previous incarnations (before he became a part time Greek plumber!).

Snippets from Correspondence

Halki Tourist shop *from Mary Lambell*

"We particularly like to visit 'off-the beaten track' places."

Changing Times - *from Jenny Booth*

...We liked Petra (Lesvos) and one of my memories is seeing an old chap wandering the streets with an enormous pile of wares - only to realise there was a donkey underneath! A far cry from the old chap on Santorini seen answering his mobile phone whilst riding his donkey.

We had a wonderful holiday this year, but I have very mixed feelings about Alonissos. Hard to put my finger on why, but I think it has something to do with the 'new' money coming in. There seems to be a danger that the character of islands could be spoiled as they cater for ex-pats and wealthy Greek holiday makers. But then these thoughts make me feel guilty - who am I to want the Greeks to stay in a 'time warp'?

I don't believe any of us want our Greek friends to be denied the conveniences and luxuries of modern day life, but we do hope that will not spoil the old traditions and ways which can still exist alongside. It is often the 'ex-pats' who build in stone or renovate old houses in villages where locals go for the modern cement option! Ed

Cretan Doggy Guide *from John Sheppard Fidler*

We were provided with descriptions of some walks among nearby Cretan mountain villages by our tour operator. We drove to the start of one and parked beside a Spring, near Argiroupoulos, south of Almiros Bay. The village, though obviously thriving, seemed deserted. While putting on our heavier shoes we noticed a medium sized sloe-eyed yellow dog had joined us, sitting beside the road nearby. As soon as he saw we were ready to start, he crossed the road and, making sure we were following, kept perhaps 5 metres ahead down the steep stone path.

After a while we came to the site of a chapel with some ancient tombs cut into the rocks up a short track. The dog sat while we made the detour to look around, waiting until we were ready to go on our way again. He stayed with us, friendly but slightly detached, guiding us for the whole walk.

Upon our return to the car 'our' dog was joined by several of his friends who greeted both him and us with equal enthusiasm, one small one insisting on sitting on our knees as we tried to change our shoes again. We saw no one in the village, but, although the people were obviously busy that day, we were impressed that they had sent their dogs to look after us in their absence. We put it down to natural Cretan hospitality.

Who Goes Where - Tour Operator Destinations

REGION / ISLAND	Airport (Yes or Close)	Abroad Holidays	Alternative Travel Group	Airtours	Amathus	Argo Holidays	Best of Greece	Club Pavillion	Cosmos/Archers	CV Travel	Direct Greece	Elysian Holidays	Explore Worldwide	Filoxenia	First Choice	Freedom of Greece	Golden Sun Holidays	Greece & Cyprus Travel	Greece Rediscovered	Greek Chapters	Greek Islands Club
Supporter details on page		85	×	×	×	16	109	11	×	×	35	×	×	139	25	×	×	65	30	×	×
IONIAN																					
Corfu*	Y	U		R	U	R	R		R	R	R			U	R		R	U	R	U	R
Ithaca/Ithaki		U								R				U						U	R
Kefalonia	Y	U		R	U	R	R							R	U		U	U	U	U	R
Kithira*		U												R	U		U				
Lefkada/Lefkas	C	U									R				R		R	U	U		R
Meganissi		U																			
Paxos* /Antipaxos		U				U	R			R		R			U					U	R
Zakynthos/Zante	Y	U		R	U	R			R		R			U	R	U	R	U			
MAINLAND									R												
Athens	Y	U			R	R	R							R	U		U		U	U	
Halkidiki, Thessaloniki	Y	U		R	U	U	R							U	R	U	R	U			
Mountains & Central		U	R											R	U				U		
Pelion & E.Coast*	Y	U	R				R							U							
Peloponnese	Y	U	R			U	R	R	R		R		R	U	RU	U	R	U	U	U	U
Thrace	Y	U												U							
West Coast (eg Parga)	Y	U									R			U	R		U		U		
N & NE AEGEAN ISLANDS																					
Chios*	Y	U										U		U		U		U			
Fourni		U																			
Ikaria	Y	U													U						
Lesvos/Mytilene	Y	U		R							R			U	R		R				
Limnos	Y	U																U			
Samos	Y	U												U		U	U	U			
Samothrace		U												U							
Thassos		U												U				R	U		
SPORADES																					
Alonnissos		U			U	U				R		U			U				U		R
Skiathos	Y	U		R	U	R	R			R			U		R	U	R	U	U		R
Skopelos		U			U	R	R			R			U			U	U		U	U	R
Skyros*		U										U		U				U			

*Plus specialists to :
CORFU -Bridge to Corfu, Something Special, **Travel with Friends (p21)**
PAXOS - Paxos Magic Holidays, **Planos Holidays (p108)**,
CHIOS - Stonelink Cottages & Heart to Art (p64)

R-Resident Representative available, U-Unescorted or local Agent contact

	Greek Options	Greek Sun	Greek Tourism-Travel	Headwater	Hidden Greece	Island Wandering	Islands of Greece	JMC	Kosmar	Laskarina	Libra/Pricenight	Manos	Olympic Holidays	Ramblers	Saga	Simply Simon	Simply Travel	Skopelos Villas	Solos	Sunvil	Tapestry	Thomsons/Portland	Travel a la Carte	Travelux	Walks Worldwide	Waymark
	x	x	42	112	80	47	x	x	x	x	x	0i:c	x	x	x	x	x	65	x	24	113	x	48	x	x	x
IONIAN																										
Corfu*		U				U		R	R			R	R	R			R		R	R		R	R		R	
Ithaki		U	R			U						R	R				R			R	R					
Kefalo	R	U	R			U		R	R			R	R				R		R	R	R	R				
Kithira		U				U								R												
Lefkad	R	U				U		R	R			R	R	R			R		R	R					RU	
Megar		U										R					U									
Paxos	U	U				U			R			R	R				R			R			R			
Zakyn	U	U				U		R	R			R	R				R		R			R				
MAINLAND																										
Athens		U	U		U	U	U	U							R	U	RU		U	U						
Halkid		U				U		R	R		R		R		R		R					R				R
Mount		U	U			U								R	R		R								RU	R
Pelion		U	R						R			R					R			R	R				R	
Pelopo	R	U	R	U	U	U			R			R	R	R			R			R						
Thrac		U				U																				
West C		U				U		R	R			R	R	R			R			R					RU	
N & NE AEGEAN ISLANDS																										
Chios		U	U		U	U																				
Fourn		U	U		U	U																				
Ikaria		U	U		U	U				R				R						R						
Lesvo		U			U	U	R	R			R	R				R										
Limno		U	U			U													R							
Samos		U	U			U	R	R	R	R	R	R		R			R			R		R				R
Samot		U				U																				
Thass		U				U	R	R			R	R					R					R				
SPORADES																										
Alonni		U				U	U			R		R	R				R			R			U			
Skiath		U				U	R	R	R			R	R				R	R	U	R	R	R	R			
Skope		U				U	U	R	R	R	R	R	R				R	U		R	R	R	U			
Skyro		U				U						R														

Plus specialists to :
KYTHIRA - **Greek Experience - Accommodation & Activity Holidays (p20)**
SKYROS - Skyros Holistic Holidays
PELION - **Houses of Pelion (p73)**

REGION / ISLAND	Airport (Yes,Close)	Abroad Holidays	Alternative Travel Group	Airtours	Amathus	Argo Holidays	Best of Greece	Club Pavillion	Cosmos/ Archers Tours	CV Travel	Direct Greece	Elysian Holidays	Explore Worldwide	Filoxenia	First Choice	Freedom of Greece	Golden Sun Holidays	Greece & Cyprus Travel	Greece Rediscovered	Greek Chapters	Greek Islands Club
Evvia		U										U	R	U						U	
ARGO SARONIC																					
Aegina		U															R	U	R		
Agistri		U																			
Hydra		U					R							U				U	U	U	
Poros		U						R										U	U	U	
Spetses		U					R			R						U		U		U	
CYCLADES																					
Amorgos		U																			
Anafi		U																			
Andros		U				R							R		U	U		U			
Astypalea		U														U					
Donoussa		U																			
Folegandros		U																			
Ios		U				R										U		U			
Iraklia		U																			
Kea (Tzia)		U											R							U	
Kimolos		U																			
Kithnos		U											R								
Koufonissi		U																			
Milos	Y	U														U					
Mykonos	Y	U		U		R	R						U		U	R	U	R	U	U	U
Naxos	Y	U	R			R									R	U	U		U	U	
Paros/ Antiparos		U					R	R					U	R	U	U	U	R	U	U	U
Santorini / Thira	Y	U		U		R	R		R		R	U	R	U	R	U	R	U	U	U	U
Schinoussa		U																			
Serifos		U																			
Sifnos		U												U							
Sikinos		U																			
Syros		U											U	R	U				U		U
Tinos		U			U								U	R			U		U		
Crete *	Y	U	R	R	U		R		R	R	R	U	R	U	R	U	R		U	U	R

*Plus specialists to CRETE: Cachet Travel (now also to SAMOS), Catherine Secker, Discover Crete, Freelance, **Martin Shepherds Crete (p18)**, Prestige, **Pure Crete (p19)**, Smart Holidays.

	Greek Options	Greek Sun	Greek Tourism-Travel	Headwater	Hidden Greece	Island Wandering	Islands of Greece	JMC	Kosmar	Laskarina	Libra/Priceright	Manos	Olympic Holidays	Ramblers	Saga	Simply Simon	Simply Travel	Skopelos Villas	Solos	Sunvil	Tapestry	Thomsons/Portland	Travel a la Carte	Travelux	Walks Worldwide	Waymark
Evvia		U				U									R				R							
ARGO SARONIC																										
Aegina		U				U			R		R	R							R							
Agistri		U				U			R			R														
Hydra		U		U		U											R									
Poros		U				U			R										R							
Spetse		U		U		U						R														
CYCLADES																										
Amorgos	U	U		U		U										U				R						
Anafi	U	U																								
Andro		U		U		U			R											R						
Astypalaia	U	U				U										U										
Donou	U	U		U		U																				
Folegandros	U	U		U		U										U										
Ios		U				U										U										
Iraklia		U		U		U																				
Kea (T		U														U										
Kimolos		U				U										U										
Kithnos		U				U								R		U										
Koufor		U		U		U																				
Milos	U	U				U										U										R
Mykonos	U	U				U	U		R		R	R	R			U		R								
Naxos	U	U		U	U	U	U		R							U				U						
Paros	U	U		U		U	U		R			R				U				U						
Santor	U	U		U		U	U	R	R		R	R	R			U	R									
Schind	U	U		U		U																				
Serifos	U	U				U								R		U										
Sifnos	U	U				U										U										
Sikinos	U	U														U										
Syros	U	U				U										U										
Tinos	U	U				U										U										
Crete	R		U	R	U	U	U	R	R			R	R	R	R		R	U	R	R		R				R

R-Resident Representative available, U-Unescorted or Local Agent contact

REGION / ISLAND	Airport (Yes,Close)	Abroad Holidays	Alternative Travel Group	Airtours	Amathus	Argo Holidays	Best of Greece	Club Pavillion	Cosmos/ Archers Tours	CV Travel	Direct Greece	Elysian Holidays	Explore Worldwide	Filoxenia	First Choice	Freedom of Greece	Golden Sun Holidays	Greece & Cyprus Travel	Greece Rediscovered	Greek Chapters	Greek Islands Club
DODECANESE																					
Agathonissi		U																			
Arki, Marathi		U																			
Halki		U									R										
Kalymnos		U				R					R						U	U	U		
Karpathos	Y	U															U	U			
Kassos	Y	U																			
Kastellorizo		U																	U		
Kos	Y	U		R	U	R					R					R	U	R	U	U	
Leros		U															U	U	U		
Lipsi		U																U			
Nissiros		U																			
Patmos		U										U		U			U				
Rhodes*	Y	U		R	U	R	R		R		R					R	U	R	U	U	
Symi		U			U	U	R										U	U	U		
Telendos		U																	U		
Tilos		U																	U		
Island Hopping/Tailored		U				U	U	U		R						U	U	U	U	U	
Touring (Land bases)		R	R	U			R		R							R	U	U		R	
Cruising (sleep on board)		R		R	R	R	R									R	R	U			
Sailing/Water Sports		U							R	R											
Walking Holidays		R	R													R	R	U			
Other Activity Holidays*		R															R			R	
FLIGHT ONLY BKGS		U		U		U										U	U	U	U	U	

Plus Specialist Activities Companies:

SCHEDULED FLIGHTS: British Airways, EasyJet, **Olympic Airways (p163)**
SAILING &/or CRUISING: Club Vassiliki, Nautilus Yachting, Neilsons, **Odyseus Yachting (p28)**, Royal Olympic Cruises, Sailing, **Seafarer (p41)**, Sunsail, **Swan Hellenic Cruises (p77)**, **Templecraft Yacht Charter (p28)**, Voyages Jules Verne.
CITY BREAKS (Athens): Bridge Travel Services, Crystal Cities, Travelscene, Travelsphere (& coach tour)
NATURE &/or WALKING: David Sayers Travel, Equitour Horse Riding, Limosa Bird Watching (Lesvos & Thrace), Natural History Travel, NatureTrek (Crete,Lesvos,Samos), Peregrine.
ANCIENT GREECE TOURS: Journey Through Ancient Greece (p141)

	Greek Options	Greek Sun	Greek Tourism-Travel	Headwater	Hidden Greece	Island Wandering	Islands of Greece	JMC	Kosmar	Laskarina	Libra/Priceright	Manos	Olympic Holidays	Ramblers	Saga	Simply Simon	Simply Travel	Skopelos Villas	Solos	Sunvil	Tapestry	Thomsons/Portland	Travel a la Carte	Travelux	Walks Worldwide	Waymark
DODECANESE																										
Agatho		U			U																					
Arki		U			U																					
Halki		U			U					R			R										R			
Kalym		U			U	U			R	R		R	R	R												
Karpa	U	U				U																				
Kasso	U	U																								
Kastell		U			U	U																				
Kos		U			U	U			R	R		R	R	R	R					R			R			
Leros		U			U	U				R				R	R											
Lipsi	U	U			U	U				R																
Nissiro		U			U	U																				
Patmo	U	U			U	U				R				R			R			U						
Rhode		U			U	U		R	R			R	R	R		R				R		R				
Symi		U			U	U			R	R		R	R	R		R							R			
Telend		U			U	U						R														
Tilos		U			U	U				R																
Island		U	RU		U	U	U	R									U			U					RU	
Tourin	U		R		U									R	R				U	U					RU	
Cruisin			R					R					R	R						R		R			RU	
Sailing			RU																	R					RU	
Walkin	R		R	R							R			R			R		R	RU		R	R		RU	R R
Other			R								R						R			R			R	R	R	
FLIGH		U					U	U	U			U	U			U	U			U		U		U		

R-Resident Representative available, U-Unescorted or local Agent contact

***Plus specialists to RHODES:** South Coast Safaris - 4x4 safaris*

*We have endeavoured to include all the **main** UK tour operators and **Greek Holiday specialists**, some trade under several brochure names (not all included) but there are many more small companies who arrange holidays to specific parts of Greece.*

Information quoted is of planned destinations for Summer 2003 - most companies do not vary their itineries significantly from one year to the next. For more details on advertised companies see page numbers indicated top row first page of chart.

Life in Greece

In this section we explore life in Greece, as observed by the visitor or from research, plus the joys, pitfalls and regulations for becoming a part of that life.

First some observations contributed by artist Mary Potter from her 'Greek Notebook'.

The Village Shop - To Pandopoleo *by Mary Potter*

At first sight the village shop seems to contain nothing, but after a few visits one comes to the conclusion that it contains everything, even though many items are covered in dust and tucked away in a dark corner. It is rightly called in Greek το παντοπωλείο - the everything shop.

The art of display is not given much priority. Why bother when everyone knows you have it and they have only to ask for it? How long it may have been on the shelves is anyone's guess. How many times the cat may have slept on it no one knows, but it is there. From a stamp to a bag of flour, to a length of material to make one's husband a new pair of trousers, to a brass table lamp to give to a niece when she gets married.

But the shop is more than a place to buy things. The well worn if uncomfortable chair is always occupied; by someone merely wanting to pass the time and talk over what's going on, or someone waiting for a telephone message from a relative, or the village priest will occupy it, or perhaps simply someone sheltering there from the rain or for a rest on his way home from work.

There may be fresh flowers on the counter, perhaps photographs of relatives behind, or of the president - I have never seen a photograph of the former royal family anywhere. Prices are written up on scraps of paper in pencil. Stocktaking - impossible, surely?

Premises can be a front parlour converted, or a lofty outhouse. Shop hours are something decided by how long the shopkeeper feels like staying open, or how busy he thinks he is likely to be.

Village shop on Tilos

These shops seem the epitome of Greek village life - friendly and inefficient.

We continue with another observation from Mary about getting involved in the everyday activities of friends in Greece and overleaf more on the same subject from Margery & Eddie Dowle.

Work or Play (1) *by Mary Potter*

We often seem to get involved in village activities, such as wine making or the distilling of raki. On our walks we come across whole families busy treading their grapes. Greeks seem to have a talent for combining work with enjoyment, even with hard work in hot weather.

Sometimes the set up is quite primitive, consisting of a pen of grapes with two men, clad only in old shorts, walking around in circles with grapes up to their knees, and often with the sweat pouring off them and surrounded by wasps. The women will be organising the boiling of the honey, presumably to sweeten the wine. An overhead pipe will be carrying the grape juice into the outhouse, to be eventually stored in huge, often beautifully hand made barrels. At least that is how the process appears to us.

The making of raki seems more complicated. For one thing the whole process takes at least two days and nights. Again a family affair, with inspectors seeing that only the two families allowed by law, are distilling it in each village. The fires that burn under these dalek-like containers with long noses, are kept stoked up for the required time, and baked potatoes done in the cinders are a delicious by-product.

From the other end of this contraption the precious liquid trickles out. Here again the law steps in, laying down the amount of water that must be added - not much, judging by the strength of the drink given us in tiny glasses and considering that the raki is made from the dregs of the already crushed grapes.

Work or Play (2) *by Margery & Eddie Dowle*

Margery & Eddie are regular visitors to their favourite Greek destination, first discovered as package tourists. Now they are retired they are able to travel freelance and spend longer periods enjoying 'Greek life' rather than being 'on holiday'.

This year was our tenth visit to stay at 'Karidia' just outside Skala Eressos, Lesvos. We stayed for 5 weeks in May/June and realised that we are no longer tourists, spending all day long on the beach as we used to. We share many happy hours sitting under the enormous walnut tree - the *karidia (καρυδιά)* hence the name of the studios - chatting, helping Gavrile (Γαβριήλ), or drinking coffee. We communicate in our mix of Greek, French, English and sign language and laugh at our mistakes. We call it Karidia International! The magic of the tree always works.

On arrival we are always greeted by Gavrile and his wife Despina (Δέσποινα) who has cooked a meal for us to eat under the tree. Tired and full of her always marvellous cooking, we wander around the large gardens that surround the small block of studios and rooms. His fruit trees, vegetables, grapevines, 6 hens, 4 turkeys and 2 sheep keep him busy every day. We too feel part of the family and help preparing crops for storage. Sometimes we go with him to his olive grove where he checks every tree. We help pick oregano which grows wild here and smells delightful as you drive along with the windows open. The stems are later sorted and tied into bundles and hung under the lower branches of the *karidia* tree to dry. A few weeks later we help remove the oregano from the stems and rub it to fill a large sack for winter cooking and for friends, family and regular holiday guests to take home. Our suitcase smells wonderful!

Work or Play?

Early in June, after we'd had many meals with fresh *koukia* (Κουκιά) - broad beans cooked in various ways, Gavrile said the beans were 'finished'. We puzzled

over this as only half his crop had been harvested. He cut down the rest and put them on a large polythene sheet on the ground behind the apartment block to dry in the sun. When the pods were completely dry we saw

Sketches by Margery Dowle

him one day, trampling on them, beating them with sticks, or with arms raised in the air. The foliage was lifted up and thrown into the wind allowing the beans to be released onto the sheet. The discarded pods are fed to the sheep - nothing is wasted here. Handfuls of beans were placed in a shallow tin, tipped gently to allow the wind to separate them from any further residue and finally the beans were stored in sacks until needed. Before cooking the eye of each bean must be removed - quite tricky, but done with ease by Despina. We now eat *Koukia* with much more appreciation of all the work involved. Gavrile's fruit and vegetables are truly organic.

Last year on arrival in September we saw that our German friends (who had been there July and August) had brought in a cable drum, left on the roadside after some street lights had been newly cabled. They had helped paint it bright yellow with all their names on it in Greek blue, and placed it under the walnut tree - a new bar!

On top of the bar were several large pumpkins harvested by Gavrile. For fun they had drawn faces on the pumpkins. On returning from the beach later we found Despina stirring what looked like chipped potatoes in a bucket of white liquid. We watched totally mystified. Despina tried in her fast Greek to explain, but we didn't understand. As I turned I saw half a pumpkin. Despina had cut the other half into pieces and that, I realised, was what was being stirred in white liquid - for 3 hours. Next the creamy white pieces were thoroughly washed and the white liquid was used to paint the bottom of the tree. Two days later the trunk was bright white. Curiouser and curiouser! The Greek explanation sounded like *'asvestos'* which worried us.

The pumpkin pieces were next cooked in a large pan with a little water and a lot of sugar for one and a half hours. When cooled the pieces are crispy on the outside and inside very soft, suspended in a golden orange very sweet syrup. Perhaps the *asvesti* (lime whitewash, I've since heard it described as) draws excess water from the fruit pieces to make them more crispy. They are served with a glass of water after coffee - another fine delicacy to offer friends (although one is enough for me!). On our sad day of departure we were presented with a well wrapped package of these *'glyka'* - a delicious reminder of our second home.

Our Year on Symi *by Tony Robinson*

Tony had just taken early retirement and as their son was in his final year of primary education, he and his wife felt this would be their last chance for some years to realise their dream of 'living' for a while in Greece.

In September 1993 my wife Anna, our 10-year old son Ben and I set off on a great adventure - a year on a Greek island.

The idea had occurred a year or two previously on the island of Halki when Anna was talking to some local women about conditions in the winter months. Before long we began to think how wonderful it would be to actually live there rather than just be tourists passing through. We chose Symi because although small it is fairly close to Rhodes airport, ferries and other facilities.

We arrived at Rhodes airport to find it was too windy for the boat to take us to Symi that day. The taxi driver confirmed this and recommended a characterful, cheap hotel in town, even coming in with us to explain our situation and ensure we were able to get a room for the night.

Next day we arrived on Symi and found Gabrielle, the English girl married to a local man, who had been so helpful in finding us accommodation. We had a lovely house, close to the main square and even had our own garden.

After a few weeks the local population realised that we were not going to go away. The days seemed to fly past; teaching Ben with the aid of numerous text books lent by his school; shopping at the various idiosyncratic little shops, in particular Yianni's lovely little 'supermarket' which we were hardly ever allowed to leave without being presented with something extra - chocolate for Ben, wine or some little delicacy; exploring the island, taking picnics to the rocks near the little bay of Nos and taking numerous photographs.

In November we were warned that everything would close down once the final tourist disappeared. Certainly a lot of places did close, but the food shops and one or two cafes along the front such as

Solitary fishing boat at dawn

Elpida's and Pacho's stayed open, also Dimitri's 'Mr Tasty' taverna opened fairly often in the evenings and other tavernas occasionally, so it was rarely a problem. We found there were good supplies of food. We were able to buy plenty of fruit and vegetables, as well as feeding regularly on stuffed peppers, kalamari, lamb and pork chops, cheese, yoghurt, olives and so on. Some days there was fish available from the harbourside and the bakers opened almost every day. We certainly didn't starve.

November also brought with it a defining moment in our stay on Symi; our meeting with the remarkable Hugo. We had read about him a year or two previously in a guidebook, wherein he was described as 'an eccentric Englishman walking around with a Harrod's bag'. Eccentric? Maybe, but in a world of such eccentricity he seemed to represent sense and sensibility. Englishman? Not entirely, for he is part Swedish on his mother's side. As for the Harrod's bag, the only bag he was carrying when he first introduced himself to us was an unassuming bag full of brown bread, available one day per week at one of the bakeries. Hugo has lived on Symi since 1977, I think, and is a fountain of local information. He takes guided walks on the island in the tourist season and knows every plant, person, track and chapel. He is also charming, amusing and generous. In short, a lovely man. He has a dog, bizarrely named Mitsubishi, who can read. At least that was our conclusion when we met Hugo off the boat one day and Mitsubishi bounded to the shore and immediately leapt on to the back of a pick-up truck which had her name emblazoned on the back! Also in my subjective judgement, Hugo writes the world's most interesting Christmas letter.

A day or two after our first meeting, Hugo arrived at our house to announce that the next day, November 25th, was St. Catherine's Day. He invited us to accompany him to St. Catherine's chapel for the celebration, suggesting we meet up in the High Town at 9am. It was a lovely sunny morning and we got to the meeting place 8.55am and sat on a wall by the kiosk waiting until about ten past when Hugo emerged from the depths of a cafe, accompanied by Kathy, an American artist staying on the island for the winter.

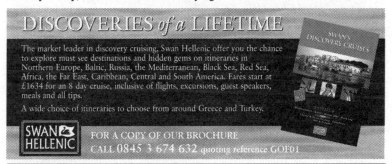

He lead us through a maze of narrow streets and alleyways, past the fire station, church and a mill wheel by a former taverna until we reached a track which overlooked the town, where we stopped to take in the views and for Hugo to have a slug of the local firewater. Then onwards along an old donkey track, up to the road, along a little way to another track which led past an orchard and to the chapel, privately owned by the same family since the 14th century.

Unsure what to expect, we entered the courtyard. There were people all around; some sitting, some standing, all waiting for the service to end. It had begun at 8 and now it was nearly 10.30. We made a donation and took candles into the tiny packed chapel, then went outside to sample Hugo's firewater and await developments. Soon the priest in his purple robes led the procession out of the chapel. There were numerous chants of 'Lord have mercy' and the like, and finally the service was over. We were offered heavily incensed bread, coffee, cakes and invited to help ourselves to brandy. Out of about a hundred people, as far as we could tell, we were the only non-Greeks. Then chairs and tables appeared, but not enough. We were invited to a table and some men went to fetch huge logs for us to sit on. We had chick pea soup, salty fish, salad and bread with red wine. After lunch we shook hands with Kosta, the owner, and made our way back to town with Kathy and Hugo. Everyone had been so friendly and hospitable - a very memorable and moving day.

By the end of November the weather was starting to change and we had the first real rain we had experienced in Greece. Storms occurred from time to time throughout the winter, invariably turning the steps outside our house into a cataract, but it soon cleared and most days there was some sunshine. One sad entry in my diary around this time reads, 'it's 2.30pm, it's raining and the kitten has died.' Hyacinth was a scrawny flea-ridden creature who hung around with some of the other cats who frequented the area around our house. She lay on the steps by our upstairs shower room, clearly losing the fight. I brought her some milk, but she had no more strength, so I just sat with her briefly as her life ebbed away.

There were many other cats, three of which clearly felt they owned the house. They had been named by the previous tenants - the mother, Problem Sue, and two sons Aesos Hellenikos and Psili Ammos. Problem Sue introduced herself to us by bringing a 'welcome gift' of a snake onto our terrace. Anna threw a bucket over it and released it into the undergrowth later when the cats were out of the way. Luckily the habit did not last long. Sadly Problem Sue fell awkwardly one day when jumping from our balcony and we never saw her again. The other two stayed all year, probably the only cats I've ever been fond of. Ben gave names to most of the cats around. The alleged father of our two was Long John, a one-eyed, roguish, piratical thug who caused us great amusement one day at a nearby taverna when he chased another cat up a tree. Being more Stan Laurel than Olga Korbut, he lost his balance on a narrow branch and landed heavily in the middle of a table occupied by shocked day-trippers from Rhodes. Food and cutlery flew everywhere and Long John beat a hasty retreat. *"Waiter, there's a cat in my Greek salad!"*

Another great character on Symi was Nico from the Symi Sponge Centre, a man fluent in several languages. He seemed to be at the heart of all Symi's social life - carnivals, festivals and he also ran the Chess Club and the cinema. It was November when we first saw adverts for films shown in the old town hall most Friday and Saturday nights out of season. The chess took place at the same venue for a couple of hours before Nico showed the videos on a big screen. As the films were mostly in English with Greek subtitles, we started to go regularly, and despite being by far the youngest there, Ben started to go to chess too. Nico became really proud of Ben's chess playing. It only cost 100 drachmas to watch the films and as we had no television, it was particularly enjoyable for Ben to be able to play chess and to watch a film, even if they weren't always to our taste.

Christmas on Symi was refreshingly low-key. One or two shops reopened for a day or so, a few decorations appeared a couple of days before and the town's tannoy system pumped out a few carols. We had one young carol singer on Christmas Eve, lamb chops for Christmas dinner and Ben's older

brother Mark came out to stay with us, so the family were all together. Early in January Mark had to return. We decided to spend a few days in Rhodes before seeing him off at the airport. The weather was superb, the beach an empty contrast to the wall-to-wall sunbeds of summer, the old town eerily deserted

The Symi I - our link with Rhodes

but for a few cafes and tavernas still open.

1994 sped along and soon Symi was once again cleaning and decorating for the tourist season. By the end of March a handful of day-trippers were arriving each day from Rhodes. In early April, one lovely sunny morning we took a picnic to Aghia Marina, a little beach about 2 hours or more walk away over the hills, beyond the windmills. The only other person around was a man valiantly clearing the beach of winter debris. Then, as if from nowhere, a figure appeared in the distance and approached the man on the beach. There was clearly a communication failure and the man was directed towards where we sat on the rocks.

He was a young, extremely courteous German tourist who had somehow become hopelessly lost. He had come from Rhodes for the day with friends, but lost his way in the High Town and thought he was near the harbour. He asked if the boat left from here. Anna said it did, but not until next *month* at the earliest! He had 10 minutes before his boat was due to leave Yialos - 2 hours walk away. As he set off up the track, the boat came round the headland and glided into the distance. We came across him that evening, happier once he had found a room for the night and been in touch with his friends.

Also in April was another defining moment. We met Aruni Constantinidi. We were having coffee at Elpida's by the harbourside when Anna noticed an advert for art classes. As she read it Aruni appeared, she was the art teacher. Within no time she was a firm friend - volatile, vivacious, generous, highly strung, intelligent and great company. We had many meals at her house. She and Anna set up an art exhibition. She had ambitious plans for a Symi International Art School. Ben even attended her art lessons at the local school. One evening she took us to a taverna in the High Town where we met a Symi-Australian family who had lived in Melbourne. It was an evening of music and signing. It was here we witnessed a man pick up a table in his teeth. At one point someone asked the emigrants what they missed most. Without hesitation they all replied 'the light'. Aruni left at the end of June to teach at Bergen University in Norway, returning shortly before our departure. We have stayed in touch.

Another abiding memory for Ben and I is watching the World Cup finals that summer - especially at the place we called, with typical Greek originality, 'The World Cup Bar' run by a lovely man from Kalamata who rarely ac-

Tony & Ben - Yialos harbourside stroll

Our Symi

Trotting down the Kali Strata,
only three hundred steps to go,
we stop to gaze and take account;
an old, eroded woman shuffles out
of a narrow, cooler alley.
Our eyes meet,
hers secure in her ancient culture,
pride burning in their very gaze.
"Kali mera" she says, and drifts
towards another unseen opening;
she knows her life
the being and the meaning.
Below the harbourside
ripples in the glare.
Midday, and the boats are in,
spilling their cargoes
of one-day snoopers
who bustle and sweat
in the steamy bowl.
The 'Triton'
has disappeared from view,
sailing to a calmer world,
strolling through the gentle seas
of unimagined blue.
Briefly, our level is deserted,
save for a calendar cat
on a bright white wall.
A man in flowered, garish shirt
of dreadful pinkness
turns to his pursuing tribe:
"Here! Here!" he yells,
and his Nikon is poised to strike
another unreal blow for posterity.
We pass him by,
resentful of his presence,
as if this barren dazzling isle
were ours,
as if we belonged.
Somewhere in time, maybe we do,
and we linger in our descent,
wishing that the time were now.

cepted our money and almost always provided food to nibble at 1 or 2 in the morning as he, Ben and I, plus sometimes one or two others, sat by the still waterside on balmy Symi nights watching our favourite game.

There are so many memories. I've not even mentioned Easter. Greek Easters are well documented with their noise, celebration, fireworks and dynamite. We never worked out where the dynamite came from, despite searching the remotest shelves of Yianni's shop where almost anything else could usually be found.

Suffice to say that one day we shall return again to that dazzling wild rock, where the days sparkled and shone, where we lived out a dream, where we felt so alive.

Komboloi - The Greek Worry Beads *by Terry Cook*

For years Greek men have carried, flicked and swung their Komboloi (κομπολόι), a string of 'worry' beads which they swirl around their hands or fiddle with their fingers. The habit is on the increase with young and old Greeks, taking comfort from the reassuring 'clack' as the beads rhythmically hit against each other.

The exact history of the Komboloi in Greece is not known for sure, but although modern komboloi have no religious significance, they almost certainly derived from prayer beads. In eastern countries the tradition goes back many centuries, and the earliest forms were actually strings of knots. The Greek word originates from *'kombos'*, which meant a knot or junction, and *'loi'* which was used for a group or line, or others say from *'leo'*, which meant to say. First used in a religious connotation by the Buddhists around the 6th Century BC as an aid to prayer, both the Hindus around the first century AD and the Moslems 500 years later adopted a similar technique.

The faithful counted their prayers on each knot or bead, and sometimes had 'multiplier' knots for reciting their devotions a certain number of times during the day. In the Christian faith, early monastic devotees are recorded as using a 33-knotted cord around the 4th century AD. Eight hundred years later the Spanish monk Dominic adopted the principle after a friend returned from the East with samples of oriental prayer rosaries.

It seems that whenever there was a need to concentrate the minds of humble men on higher things, finding both an aid to counting off rituals and providing a distraction for the hand was a goal satisfied by the ring of beads. Orthodox monks in northern Greece were using knotted ropes as an aid to devotions in the middle ages, and around the 15th century the Catholic Church introduced the 150-bead Rosary.

There are various interpretations of the origin and popularity of komboloi in Greece today. Theories include a 'mimicking' of the Muslim Turkish former rulers, trying to detract from the religious meaning the Turks placed on the beads. Another proposes the idea that the Turkish overlords did not want the Greeks shaking hands with each other, since it would have been too much encouragement for their unity and national pride, so they gave them the strings of beads to occupy their hands!

Or maybe the Greek men so burdened with the trials and distresses of life after years of oppression and deprivation, just discovered one day the relaxation that the touch, the sound and companionship of the beads afforded. Different in style from earlier 'religious' strings, the Komboloi of the Greeks had a space on the string enough to go over the hand, and enable the beads to be swung. These strings were designed much more for the movement, the feel and the sound.

Typically the Komboloi has about 23 beads, although the number is not important, since it is not used to count anything specific. The size of the hand, the overall length preferred and the shape and diameter of the beads tend to determine how many are used. The feature of the Greek Komboloi was more that it just goes on and on and on. Historically the most treasured are the natural amber, some say because when smoothed and polished, it's the most natural feel of all substances.

Faturan ('manufactured' amber from the filings as solid amber beads were shaped and honed), from Egypt also became very popular. The tradition of manufacture was a closely guarded secret, and would be passed from father to son by word of mouth and demonstration. Traditional Komboloi made by craftsmen in prized materials can command very high prices indeed, and the purist would despise all the modern 'commercial' imitations which abound in tourist Greece.

Apparently sales are up and it is not only to the tourists. Some Greek yuppies spend small fortunes on the latest 'designer' beads - gold, amber, mother of pearl, ivory from smart jewellery stores are as popular as the cheap plastic, wooden or metal ones from the 'periptero' kiosks. The type of beads they swing and click are a statement of their personal style.

Nowadays, it's not only the men who can be seen with the beads swinging in their hands. Women are beginning to adopt them - some as a fashion statement, but no doubt others to share the tradition, and the benefits which they bring. Melina Mercouri could often be seen fingering a silver stranded Komboloi, as she championed the cause for Greece's cultural heritage.

For whatever reason men or women take up the beads, it's probably more accurate to describe them, as one commentator has in modern parlance, 'No worry beads'. Give them a try.

If you would like more information and history on the Komboloi, visit the Komboloi Museum in Nafplion, see Aris Evangelinos' Book reviewed in this volume or the internet site at www.cs-net.gr/komboloi.

The Creature from the Blue Lagoon *by Roy Lawrance*

What's that in the sea Dad?" my daughter enquired.

"Looks like a black bin-sack to me" I replied.

"No it's not, it's going round in circles, bin-sacks don't do that".

Andromachis beach was 'our' beach; it was about an hour's walk from Sigri, on the island of Lesvos, and we usually had it to ourselves. I normally spent my time here working on an all-over body tan and today was no exception. Without hesitation, I ran naked down to the sea and plunged in to investigate what this object was doing in 'our' private bay. In my daughter's eyes I took on the role of hero as, nearing the bobbing black mass, I realised it was a sheep that was panicking even more the closer I got.

Roy Lawrance

It was obviously in the wrong environment for sheep and seemed incapable of steering itself back towards the beach. We circled each other a few times as I tried to encourage it back towards land, but all it did was keep turning its head towards me with a wide-eyed manic stare. By grabbing one of its horns we slowly began to head inshore as I fought to keep its head above water. Exhausted, and half-drowned by my hanging on to its head, the creature soon became more relaxed and we were eventually washed up on the beach like a pair of shipwrecked sailors.

Life in Greece - Creature from the Blue Lagoon

"Well done Dad!" my daughter said as she helped me pull the animal further out of the waves. I couldn't answer, breathless and exhausted I lay slumped over the mass of wet sheep trying to get my breath.

"You like sheeps?" a stranger's voice broke the air.

"Yes..., this one..., needed..., help" I replied gasping for air.

"This is boy sheeps."

"No you don't understand, it was in trouble and..." my words failed as I suddenly remembered I was stark naked.

The man introduced himself as Dimitri who, along with his extremely attractive girlfriend, was here for the day and luckily lived on the other side of the island and not in Sigri. Like all Greeks, they were modestly dressed wearing swimsuits and seemed more embarrassed than I was. Between us, we managed to drag the exhausted creature to the shade of a tamarisk tree where I shook Dimitri's hand and nonchalantly strode back to my threadbare beach mat to look for my shorts.

As the day progressed, we shared our beach and chatted about our respective lives and travel experiences. Dimitri explained that he was doing his National Service, but most weekends he was allowed off to help his Dad in their family taverna. I just hope Turkey never decides to invade Greece on a weekend.

We shared our food and Dimitri introduced us to the delights of eating live black sea urchins with a small spoon, washed down with ouzo. He dug up small sea shells for us to eat that tasted superb and warned us about the *Euphorbia* plants growing wild that lined the beaches and whose white milky sap could blind. It was a day of learning, comparing lifestyles and shared dreams, ... and an opportunity to explain why I was wrestling naked with a half-drowned sheep when they had first arrived on the beach.

"This is the best beach on the island" Dimitri confided to me.

"We have been coming here for ten years" I replied.

"To Sigri ... wow, Sigri is full of crazy people" he said in amazement.

"I know, that's why we return each year."

Building Our Dream Home - *by Sue Thompson*

In the Summer of 1988, my husband Mike and I discovered an unspoilt corner of Greece and purchased 4,000 square metres of an olive grove, within one minute's walk of a long sandy beach. We had views to die for; facing west was twelve miles of sea before the Mani peninsula rose up to Taigetos, the highest mountain in the Peloponnese which is cloaked in its snowy mantle from October to June, and to the east, a sea of olives stretching to the foothills of a small mountain ridge, Korkoula, which looks like a cardboard cutout.

We took a trailer tent with us on our first drive down there, which we left on the land that summer, so for the first few years we camped on our special place, which wasn't ideal. There was no water supply, no level place suitable for setting up camp and opening everything up, and cleaning and packing it all back again always took half a day. But we enjoyed it enormously and told ourselves *"won't it be wonderful to one day have a house here!"* I spent many happy hours drawing up plans being a frustrated architect at heart. Simplicity was the key, but we wanted it to be viable in winter as well as summer so I included a fireplace, and unlike England, it was essential to have at least one outdoor area in the shade. Working to a plan of 120 square metres including balconies, I came up with a design for a large sitting room with a kitchen corner, two bedrooms, one en-suite with a bath (very useful for washing sheets and towels) and a shower room. There would be a large northeast facing verandah accessible only through the sitting room, and a balcony around the south and west sides of the house, so we could sit and watch the setting sun over the Mani.

We had met Barbara from our nearest village, Elea, on our first *recce*, and she proved to have useful contacts - or so we thought! *"Let me introduce you to my friend Petros, who is an architect and constructional engineer, he knows all about building houses"*. Fine, we thought, but would there be a problem of communicating technical details in a foreign language? Not a bit of it. Petros had lived many years in Canada and proudly showed us his framed degrees from McGill University, one in Constructional Engineering, the other in Modern Languages. He had built several houses around Elea which he could show us and he would be delighted to build our dream house for us!

It was agreed that he would employ the builders and supervise their work, and buy the necessary materials. We would repay him at cost, and send payments at intervals directly into his account through the Greek Bank in London on receipt of his invoices. He estimated that the total cost would be 65,000 - 85,000 drachma per square metre (about £20-30 per square foot) and his charge would be 7% of the total cost. Why, at this stage, we didn't

get a contract legally drawn up, I still don't know! He also agreed to negotiate with a neighbouring farmer who had an irrigation pipe running through
part of our land, for us to have a connection from this to supply our house
with water.

Meanwhile Petros applied to our main town of Sparti for a building permit
and I drew up a final plan. Greece came belatedly to the notions of planning, but the rules now are very strict. Whilst our neighbour's house appears to be propped up by our fence, I had to narrow the design of my
original plan, because it had to be at least ten metres from the boundary!
There was also a problem that if there were a fire, a fire engine would not be
able to reach us within twenty minutes. This was obvious as the nearest
fire station was in Sparti, an hour's drive away! I never discovered how this
was resolved - but I suspect we paid for it!

Petros informed us early in 1992 that work was about to commence! We
arranged to go in August for our first inspection and were delighted. There
was a large hole in the ground with reinforced wooden shoring, and whilst
we were there, the concrete lorries came and poured vast amounts between the slats, creating the footings and house floor. The land sloped
away on the site, which meant that although the front was on ground level,
it became 'upstairs' as one walked round to the back, and the underneath
part gave us half the size of the house again, into which a large reservoir

was built for our
water supply. We
paid Petros for the
work that had been
done to date and
returned home,
comforted by the
thought that real
progress was be-
ing made.

Mike went for a
week in February the following year, to ensure that all was going well, and
to pay for more work done. We were slightly concerned that the invoices
were scraps of paper on which were scribbled rough figures, but we knew
by now that Greek ways of doing things are usually far more casual than
ours! We arranged to return at the end of June, and were very pleased to
see a house standing there. True it was only the asbestos block walls and
the roof frame, but nonetheless, recognisable as the solid form of my plan.
We chose the bathroom tiles and sanitary ware including a bath, and ensured that Petros had the details for the internal finishes. Also at this time,
we were approached by our neighbour, Panayotis. He wanted to have

electricity put in his house, would we share the cost of having it brought over from the nearest point? We gladly agreed, as we'd been prepared to pay for the whole cost of electricity brought to our house!

In October we returned, and by now the internal walls were up and all the outside work had been completed. All that was needed were the windows and door casements to be inserted in their places, and internal fixtures to be finalised. Our only cause for concern was the lack of detailed pa-

perwork, which Petros assured us *"just needed to be typed up"*. Unfortunately, he said, at our final meeting before returning home, his secretary hadn't been able to do this yet, but he would send it to us at the beginning of the following week. Obviously the money we had paid so far had been used to build the house, it was just a question of how it compared with what Petros had actually paid out. We also discussed completion dates. *"I can have it all finished for you by the end of February"* said Petros confidently. So before we flew back to England, we bought some bedroom furniture in Athens and arranged to have it delivered at a date to be arranged the following spring.

Our detailed paperwork didn't arrive, and when we could get hold of Petros, he always had some excuse whilst assuring us that progress was being made with the house. In the New Year of 1994, we started to make plans for driving down with a car load of household items all ready to take up occupation! We decided to allow an extra month for completion, and go to Greece at the end of March. We couldn't get Petros on the phone at all, so we faxed him accordingly. We received no reply from any of our faxes to him, and as February passed into March, became increasingly concerned. Should we cancel going down, or proceed as arranged? I was convinced that he would have let us know if there had been a real problem, and that no one would allow us to drive from England to an incomplete house - so much for my belief in my fellow beings!

Our final fax asked him to meet us at Barbara's restaurant the evening we would arrive, so he could give us the key. But our impatience was such, we decided to drive down to look at the house before going into the village. What a shock! The house was still without doors and windows, although the floors had been tiled but not polished, and the bathrooms had been tiled and fitted out but there was no sign of a bath! As we drove into the village in our dazed state, we realised that Petros would not be waiting for us at Barbara's. After something to eat, we booked into an hotel, and settled down to sleep, ready for the next day's battle. As we walked into Petros' office next morning, we were confronted with one very shifty-eyed Greek!

We were unable to get an explanation from him of why he had not contacted us regarding the incomplete house, just an admission that the work had been delayed. Trying to pin him down to get the necessary contractors to work on the house in the next few days whilst we were there proved pointless. *"Right"* we said, *"if you're not prepared to arrange for the work to be done, we will!"* and with that we stormed out of his office, never to return. It was interesting that his secretary sneaked out a few minutes later and caught us up on the Platia, to apologise. Apparently she wanted to reply to our communications warning us, but Petros had forbidden her so to do. Within months she left Petros and found a job elsewhere!

Since we had been going to Elea, we had become friends with Chris, a Greek-Canadian and his Swiss wife who had settled in the village with their children. Coming down this time we brought a fax machine that Chris had asked us to get for him. When we took it to him and Linda, we asked them for the names of local *'masteras'*. We'd already met the window-maker Stephanos, so that was no problem but we also needed to get the marble cleaned and polished, and to find a carpenter and electrician. Talking through the problem with our friends, they came up with a solution. They would take on the completion of the house using contractors they knew, we would pay their bills direct, and Chris and Linda would do the less skilled work like painting for so much an hour. We were a bit hesitant, but after meetings with an electrician and carpenter, and a visit to Stephanos, we *'employed'* Chris and Linda.

We had a frantic two weeks, arranging as much as we could before we returned to England. Stephanos agreed to fit the made-up window casements and doors for which we had already paid Petros, but we decided it was not worth trying to change the shower for a bath. Apparently Petros had rung the bathroom shop and actually changed our order from a bath to a shower! Chris was quite confident that he and Linda would be able to get the house finished off by the end of June, when we hoped to return, and we would keep in close touch through his new fax machine. During the next two months we had regular updates by fax, and when we returned later that summer, were delighted with what they had done for us.

Our house was virtually finished - certainly enough for us to move in! We still needed four internal doors, which later we shipped out from England at a cheaper price than it would have been for us to have one door made locally by a carpenter! There were various bits and pieces that we needed to sort out, and these we did gradually over time. Oh, but the joy of being in our house by the sea!

Problems arose, such as the fact that Petros had never actually paid Stephanos our money for the windows, nor arranged with our neighbouring farmer to supply us water, but with time we managed to sort these and other mishaps out. For the last eight years we have been glorying in our Greek home, sometimes on our own, other times with friends. Never for a moment have we regretted what we have done, indeed, we would do it again, although I suspect we would set about it differently!

Disaster & Dichotomy - by *Sylvia Cook*

It was about 1pm in UK, two days before we were to go to our Greek home for 6 weeks, when we received the telephone call *"There's no easy way to say this, your house has burned down."* said the voice calling from Lesvos.

It was an ex-policeman from Sheffield, who moved to Eressos village in February. We'd not met him yet, but we'd lent him our electric fires and sent photographs of their newly purchased home at Christmas because his wife had said to another friend she'd forgotten what it looked like. They'd only seen it for 20 minutes before agreeing the purchase. When he introduced himself saying *"you don't know me, but..."* I thought maybe he wanted us to bring something from England for them.

The last Greek-o-File quarterlies were all enveloped and waiting in 9 large post office sacks in our small dining room-cum-despatch office, ready for collection. We were sorting computer files and papers to take with us, checking the list from our Christmas visit of what to take this time - shampoo, replacement copies for a few damaged cassettes, Marmite, mustard powder, office supplies and the ticks against those items where we had plenty at the house - sun lotion, toothpaste, old t-shirts, jumpers, etc.

Terry had just got back from the office where he works part-time. The bookkeeper there had just announced she was leaving after the next day - no notice - but what could they do as she had just got confirmation of their house sale and was moving from the area. All Terry's efforts to show her what to do, what to email him at his 'virtual office' in Eressos wasted and now he would need to do their invoicing and lots more from Greece too. I didn't know this extra twist of the knife when I went through to Terry's office in the spare bedroom and said *"The worst thing that can happen, has happened to Spiti Cook - it's burnt down."* We hugged in a state of shock.

I'd asked a few questions, not many at that stage. It seems that friends of ours who water the garden sometimes when we are in the UK had gone to prepare the house, turning the power and fridge on, putting some milk, eggs and bread ready for us, thinking we would arrive on the Thursday flight. They'd gone on to another friend who knew we were coming Sunday morning, so they were returning about an hour later and saw flames through the roof and several local people already there, the gate broken down and two garden hoses aimed to prevent the spread of the fire.

We understand the local fire appliance was there before noon, but didn't work! It was not until 12.45, we were told at the fire station the next Monday when there to give statements, that the Eressos police telephoned the Kalloni fire station to request help, which took another hour to arrive, being a fair distance away. The priority was to make sure that nearby houses did not catch fire. It was already too late for Spiti Cook to be saved.

The elderly former owner had been seen at the house helping and in tears later. He and his wife had brought up 3 daughters in the two rooms and kitchen as it had been. Other friends had spent their first months together there, including their honeymoon, yet others had sat in its kitchen before our time, or at parties with us in the courtyard. Many could recall happy times at Spiti Cook. Other villagers were worried for their own houses and questions were being asked about how it happened, why the fire appliance had not worked, why nothing could be done to save the house. This was a sad day for many people.

Before 3pm local time it was all over. The friends who'd turned the power on were obviously devastated, each thinking the other had gone missing. Alekos, our local bar owner friend and 'Mr Fixit' who had seen the smoke from his back window, had run up to see what was happening - he too felt speechless, unable to tell us the bad news. I'm not sure if the ex-policeman volunteered or was volunteered but we were grateful for his call. It would have been dreadful to arrive unprepared for this shock.

Terry rang back to get more information. We got into 'action' mode. I don't think the reality had sunk in yet. We'd been told there were offers of places to stay. What else should we take now? - towels, more clothes, paper, a printer, leave behind the mustard powder and Marmite, hardly important now. We remembered the brand new colour printer we had taken out at Christmas. We'd printed those house pictures to send and been able to hand out pictures of festivities taken on the new digital camera. Although there was an ancient Amstrad and a MacIntosh computer there, we had long since upgraded to carrying portable computers back and forth to handle the greater demands of modern computer software.

As we busied ourselves, every so often we'd think of some little (or big) thing that was no more. Obviously all the furniture including Aunty Edie's fireside wing chairs which we'd only managed to get out there last year (the most comfortable chairs in Eressos!) with fond memories of Terry's aunt who had died aged 94 a few years before. Some bits and pieces from my mum's home - irreplaceable memories. Mum sadly died less than two years ago, never having seen Spiti Cook or Eressos due to her disabilities, but she'd always enjoyed looking at the photographs.

Of course we could get another dolphin rug, the one on the wall in the new basement bedroom and winter eating area, but will we find another lamp like the one on the windowsill Terry bought in Kalloni when he first moved in? It was so much a part of that view down the old cobbled street across the old tiled rooftops. There were souvenirs from our travels in Greece - the blue chicken jug from Karpathos, the rugs from Lefkada, the little seagull from Tinos perched on the shelf, the pottery and blue glass from Lesvos, books, pictures. When the armchairs had moved in last year, Terry had made a bench seat from parts of the old futon - the importation of which had been a story in itself. The mattress had gone under ours to make the bed more comfortable. All now gone. Every year there had been something new, some small change or more major ones. Spiti Cook had evolved over the years to contain far more than most Greek village houses.

We would easily find more old clothes and linens at home in Britain, things replaced before the previous ones were really worn out, still at the back of the cupboard. But the memories .... will they fade with their tangible forms now destroyed?

The next day after the shock, the replanning and activity, the reality set in. It was as if there was a big hole inside. We told Terry's daughters and a few other people who were coming out to Eressos.

But now the dichotomy. It seems that with life in Greece, more than the humdrum existence of life in Britain, there is always good and bad, *yin* and *yang*. Maybe you must pay for the good in life by something very bad happening to you. What could make up for such a devastating event on this scale?

Friends had been invited to a birthday party in Greece, my 50th. Terry's daughters had been to Spiti Cook first 10 years earlier for my 40th birthday with a few other friends. Well, for 50 we reckoned we could persuade a few more, plus we have made many friends in Eressos, so they were all primed for a party. What they did not know was that we were getting married on my birthday. It was to be a surprise and we would not tell them until they arrived in Eressos. Although planned since the previous year, having researched for a weddings article for Greek-o-File, we were not sure we'd be able to 'pull it off' on the planned day. Eressos is not set up for tourist weddings. At Christmas they had insisted we could book nothing until they had the papers - including foreign office approved, translated and Greek embassy approved documents, to say there was no impediment to our marriage, dated less than 13 weeks before the wedding date! You see the potential problem! (see p104 for full details of documents, etc.)

Anyway the documents had been sent registered a week before to Alekos, our *'koubaros'* in Eressos, so it was looking to be definite. We had to give good news with the bad, so we told Terry's girls, now aged 17 and 19. They almost seemed more emotional about the surprise wedding than the loss of Spiti Cook. We had also told the friends who'd turned on our electricity, as they desperately needed some cheering up and to know we did not hold them responsible. We had a call from another UK friend, already holidaying in Eressos, who had found out about the fire. There were mixed emotions with the good and bad news - but without the good news, I'm not sure how we would have coped with the loss of our beautiful Greek village home.

We flew over night on the Saturday, arriving at Mytilene very early Sunday morning where Giorgos met us with our hire-car. We had already reckoned we could not manage without transport for the first part of our stay whilst we had friends around. We stopped off in Kalloni for breakfast coffee and came across the Greek husband of an American-Greek girl we've known since her tour rep. days in Eressos. They had not heard about the fire yet. We arrived at Alekos' bar in Eressos village about 11.00am. He used to let rooms above and was currently renovating them, so the floor was up with fat blue tubes for electric wires snaking across the cement floor, but he said we could stay there while we sorted ourselves out. We were very grateful and accepted his offer, wanting to be with a friend and near our home. Good friends are another antidote to bad news.

We put our cases upstairs, had a welcome coffee, all the while just wanting to see the 'worst thing'. We'd heard the ironing board was still sticking up in the basement, so although we had been told the main house was totally burnt out, we kept hoping there was something to salvage. Nothing could really have prepared us for that first sight of the ruins of our dream house. As we walked up the cobbled street, round the corner, there was Spiti Cook. The walls still standing and the blue gate, but through the once blue shuttered, now burnt edged windows we could see the sky.

The firemen had left red and white striped plastic tape cordoning off the house. We untied the plastic and went inside. We climbed the strong stone steps still standing in front of the main door, now gone, and stared down inside at a

metre depth of charred rubble, bed-springs (where perhaps we would have laid resting after our journey when fire broke out), the burnt out remains of the new water heater, broken dreams. Our village neighbour had followed us inside - she speaks no English and her Greek has a heavy local dialect - but her pain was evident.

I'm glad we weren't there to see it burning, knowing we could do nothing.

And now we are picking up the pieces. We've been through all sorts of emotions and ideas. We've thought of and rejected many - forgetting Greece and Greek-o-File, or moving away from here and starting afresh in another part of Greece, or doing other work to get some money and coming back in a few years time. But what we really want is Spiti Cook back again, now. We loved the house, we love much about the area in spite of its failings, we've made many friends. We want our Greek home in Eressos village, pretty much as before outside, but inside we can make some things different, take advantage of the 'clean start'.

I didn't think when it happened that I could write about something so personal for Greek-o-File, although earlier quarterly issues contain much about our travels and personal experiences. Several readers wrote to us *'Dear Sylvia & Terry, ... I feel I already know you from reading Greek-o-File'*. We were pleased to think of our readers as like-minded friends. The personal approach was always intended - but could we really share the emotions of losing our Greek home ?

I wasn't even able to think about working on this book or do more than handling day to day emails at first, once we got the telephone and internet connections sorted at our temporary base. Then I was lying on the beach one late afternoon, after the hectic time when we'd had friends around and got married and after I'd managed to start real work again, I found myself going through the facts and the feelings we'd experienced. Then I decided that I did need to write this down. It is a kind of catharsis, a grieving process, but I also feel that those who have known us and Greek-o-File would want to know.

Friends were wonderful and we had many offers of places to stay. It was good to spend our first few nights in the village, but we had thought a move to Skala Eressou would be a good idea, at least whilst friends and Terry's girls were here, then maybe we'd go back up to the village. The delays in speaking to people and the bureaucracy soon made us realise we would not be doing much on the house during this 6 weeks, so we accepted a kind offer from a builder friend of a self-contained studio next to his in Skala where we had our telephone from the house temporarily transferred.

We brought many things cleaned up from our Spiti Cook kitchen which made us feel at home. The kitchen was a separate building alongside, and remains intact, although many plastic items melted and there is smoke damage. We dismantled the kitchen worktop to make a long desk laying across two small tables in our studio bedroom. We even installed our washing machine from the wooden 'apothiki' which was also undamaged.

Again the dichotomy - wonderful friends who care and do everything they can, sympathetic villagers who stop us and make it clear how they feel for us in long dialectic speeches we can't translate, but feel we understand - but unhelpful bureaucrats and those who are already the most wealthy people here, wanting to be made richer from our misfortunes.

We had much differing advice about what to do to rebuild/repair the house. Many said, *"just go ahead and fix it - no one will say anything because of the disaster"*. Or, *"Speak to the local chief policeman and ask him to turn a blind eye"*. We know of several cases where licences have not been sought or were incomplete and local politics mean someone who is jealous or at variance with your contacts reports it and that means more cost, more anguish, more stress. Others said help the rest of the village by going to a lawyer and sue the local council for compensation. Like 99% of people here we do not have insurance. We had been told that bad local fire cover made it unavailable or very expensive and not living here all the time meant they may not pay out if anything did happen. I remember saying, *"Well, the worst thing that could happen is the house could burn down!"*

Someone said the mayor could arrange a repair licence for us which would be cheaper because of the disaster (and perhaps because he and his team were responsible for not maintaining the fire appliance). We feel it should be possible to do things legally AND cheaply in our circumstances.

Having got all our marriage papers approved and sent in advance, with a letter in Greek confirming the details we thought we had agreed in principle on our winter visit, two days after we arrived we had to see the mayor again to finalise wedding details. He said (as he had in January) that the ceremony must be in the town hall, not the harbour. We reminded him that we had this discussion back in January. We had told him about other British people married in Lindos and Tilos (featured in Greek-o-File) and he had telephoned someone and then agreed. Getting nowhere in Greek, I decided to go for the 'sympathy vote' and said *"You do know we are the couple who lost their house in the fire?"*. He smiled sweetly, said *"Yes, he was very sorry, anything he could do"*, etc, etc. Then said if it was up to him the wedding ceremony could be anywhere. We insisted, reminding him of his earlier agreement and he made a telephone call again, then said OK! The wedding invitations we'd printed hastily in England, when we heard we had lost our printer here, would be correct after all.

So two more days later we wrote a letter in English to get translated to ask the mayor to organise a repair licence, since he had said he would *"do anything he could for us"*. There is a helpful good English speaker in the town hall who we gave the letter to and asked if he could translate it - he said *"the mayor speaks English"* ! Not when it doesn't suit him, he doesn't!

It was another two days, several attempted visits when he was not there or not free and we could have been doing other things (we could not make an appointment), when we saw him again about the repair licence. He said *"No"*, we must go to the *'mechanikos'* (the local civil engineer/ architect who draws up plans and obtains licences) and he would arrange it. By this time we had asked around and been recommended to a *mechanikos* who had not been involved in any of the recent poor work or mistakes we had heard of. We gave his name and the mayor said *"Yes he can do it"*. We asked him to telephone first, but he insisted we must see him ourselves. That was a Friday (aren't they always) so no chance of any action till next week and we were getting married on the Tuesday. We'd hoped to know we were moving forward before our big day.

It took a week of many calls and fruitless visits to set up the meeting with the recommended *mechanikos*. We'd drawn some simple plans of the minimum we would like to do and other possibilities if we could incorporate them. Because our Greek does not stretch to complicated matters, we arranged the meeting at a favourite taverna where the owner had said he knew the man and could translate for us. He arrived and proceeded to explain to Kostas what we thought were options. We listened to the translation. There was only the first option - to clear the ground and rebuild a new house, at least 6 months for a licence, minimum one year total to build and at a cost we later calculated (per sq mtr) to be more than double what Spiti Cook has already cost to purchase (twice) and renovate over the years including the land and all the taxes. This was clearly NOT an option for us and NOT what we were asking for. He claimed there was no repair licence for these circumstances. He had not asked us any questions, nor seen our plans or the site. He was not interested unless he could make money from us. It was a Friday again of course. We went back to our studio without eating that evening, not wanting to see anyone, dejected again!

We decided to 'fire on all cylinders' from then, ask everyone, try everything instead of building up our hopes and working towards one idea at a time. Two people were going to ring contacts at the Mytilene office where licences are issued on Monday. We tried the British Embassy in Athens - shut on Saturday, but we got through on Monday. A very helpful man told Terry he'd look into it and to get back the next day.

That night Terry's sister managed to fall onto a low wall sustaining a bad cut to the head, necessitating a midnight trip to the Andissa clinic for stitches then on to the hospital in Mytilene for x-rays and tests. We got there after 3am. A friend had insisted on coming with us to share the driving. Just as well, as he slept in the car while we were in the hospital and at 4.30am they said they needed to keep her in for observation overnight. Dave drove me back and Terry stayed behind not returning until the afternoon. (She was fine by the way - just not allowed to drink for the rest of her holiday!)

So I was the one who called the British Embassy contact that morning to try to make some progress. Our other attempts at finding a repair licence had drawn a blank and again people said - *"Just do it"*. The embassy man said *"On no account act without a licence - it's not worth it. They can stop the work, bulldoze anything you have done, so it would all cost much more. Local politics and jealousies are a problem here."* He recommended getting a lawyer to help. I told him what we thought of Greek lawyers from previous experiences and he gave telephone details of a new one on their books for Mytilene (we'd not used before). She not only spoke good English, but by the next day had spoken to a Mytilene *mechanikos* explaining our position. We arranged to meet him at the kafeneion near our house.

When we arrived with our builder friend, the new *mechanikos,* who is from nearby Andissa, was chatting with Alekos at the kafeneion. He'd handled Alekos' plans 20 years before when he was just starting out. He took measurements at our house and, through our two interpreters, seemed to understand exactly what we wanted and not once suggested we should start from scratch. Two days later we had a verbal quote for the licence, his fees and the initial IKA payments 1100 euros and probably another 1000 for IKA later, plus, obviously, the building materials and labour costs which we can organise and do as much as we can ourselves.

So constantly we are up and down, there is good and bad in everything.

The wedding by the way went wonderfully. We were quite pleased that the mayor had to be in Athens that day so his deputy stood in and did a grand job. We did get flowers from the town hall, placed on a table borrowed from a friend's bar. There was no charge and although we had originally intended to put some money in an envelope for the mayor's office, I'm afraid in the circumstances we didn't feel like being generous to them!

The sun shone. The strong winds of earlier in the day had died down. We and our friends gathered at the harbour in front of the little church, below Vigla Hill where in 5th century BC Sappho, her friends and family had lived and married. The deputy mayor was 15 minutes late of course (the prerogative of the bride is obviously transferred to officials in Greece), but that was really just part of the perfect day.

We all gathered around with our *'koubari'* - best man (Alekos, 'Mr Fixit' from the local kafeneion) and best woman (Stephanie, who had stayed in Spiti Cook for her own first months and honeymoon in Eressos). After the short ceremony in Greek, (English translation passed around) they signed the register with us. The champagne was opened. We turned on the radio cassette in the car - positioned to start at Tolis Voskopoulos and Marinella signing *'S'agapo'* in their sultry voices, turned up loud. Photos were taken. Then, perhaps the best bit of all and quite magical, our friend Vassilis took up his bouzouki and played, leading the wedding party back up the road,

Photograph - Paul Smithson

past the fishermen who encouraged our guests to clap along, past the villagers in Skala Eressou who stood up and clapped as we passed and on through the tavernas to our favourite one at the other end where we ate, drank and made merry with more music, signing and dancing into the night.

The best wedding we've ever been to and what better antidote to the bad things that can happen in this life.

We cleared all the burnt debris out before returning to England, with the help of Giorgos who is a bit old for shovelling these days but has a small

truck that fits in narrow streets, together with Babis a wiry 'human digging machine'. Babis had helped excavate the basement about 10 years ago and is often seen digging holes in the village whenever such a job is necessary. It was cathartic finding remnants of tools, clothes and linens. There was nothing to salvage but a few souvenirs of melted blue glass and half a small china pot Molly and Alice had given us years before. With the basement floor swept out and the courtyard tidied it felt like a new beginning - Spiti Cook will rise again from the ashes!

We haven't got the licence yet. We had hoped to before we left, but the planning office don't do much in the summer. Our builder friend is not really available until autumn so hopefully we can make a start then and maybe we'll even get to live in and complete our house from the inside this winter. We are still unable to get anything in writing.

And so the moral of this episode has to be that such wonderful things can happen in Greece - be they friendships, beautiful scenery, lazy days, gentle or more wild sociable nights - but be aware - there is a downside. There are always problems, procrastinators and unhelpful people to knock you down when life seems so perfect. Perhaps this up and down with higher highs and lower lows is better than a humdrum existence where money matters more than living and you never take chances or dare to break the mould.

* * *

Buying Property in Greece - *Summary by Sylvia Cook*

We first researched and wrote about buying property in Greece in June 1999. This issue proved to be the most popular requested when subscribers wanted just 'the odd' issue rather than the whole lot. Here we present a summary as a rough idea of the purchase costs you can expect. We understand this is still correct as at September 2002, but that tax changes which favour the buyer will probably soon be made law. Nothing can be confirmed as we go to print, but possibly the transaction tax rates will change, rather than the methods - do ask about tax changes if you are buying soon.

The price of your Greek home is generally lower than a similar size home in the UK - depending on where in Britain you are and where in Greece you are purchasing. The further inland or more difficult a place is to get to, the cheaper the sale price - but expect to pay much more in taxes and costs than the equivalent conveyancing costs in the UK. Look around at several properties in an area and compare prices before committing yourself.

Find a local lawyer and try to get an itemised estimate of costs before committing yourself to a purchase. (This can be difficult to achieve!) You can expect the following costs on top of the price you are paying the seller:

Transaction tax - Urban properties 11 - 13% of *contract purchase price**
Non urban properties 9 - 11% of contract purchase price.

Municipality Tax - 3% of the amount of the transaction tax above.

Notary's Fees (inc stamp tax, duties, contract copies etc) 2-3% of price.

Lawyer's Fees - subject to agreement. In practice far in excess of the 1% we were told to expect! You may also be expected to pay the seller's costs.

Mortgage Registry Fee - 0.3% (quoted as 4.5 o/oo - which is approx .3%!)

* The 'contract purchase price' is generally lower than the market price you are paying - unless you are buying a dilapidated house for renovation in which case it may be higher. This is a taxable value for the property based on its size and location. You should therefore get your lawyer to negotiate the lowest possible 'contract price'.

If you are carrying out **major renovations** like building an extension or putting a new roof on, you will need a **planning licence** and will have to pay **IKA** (Greek Social Security) - a bit like our employer's National Insurance, but

payable whether you hire building workers or do the work yourself! If you do not obtain a licence and display its number on the building site before work commences you can be ordered to stop work, or the authorities could even knock down the work you have done and fine you.

As a rough guideline, the architect/civil engineer's fee including licences is from about **€300 per 10 square metres**, but you will need to get a quote based on the work required. The IKA is rather more - about **€750 per 10 m²** (I think this is for a 2 storey house), maybe half that for a repair licence for a new roof being just one 'layer', but we were unable to get confirmation of how the proportional cost is calculated for repair licences. Obviously you have material and labour costs on top of that.

There are no taxes or planning licences needed for any work inside an existing home - eg for new bathrooms, kitchens, windows, plumbing, painting or woodwork.

Here are a few lessons to remember that people we have come across or we ourselves have learnt the hard way:

Lessons to Consider if You Own a Greek Home

Written Information - Get everything you can in writing, particularly when paying out large sums of money. Even if it is in Greek and you cannot translate it, someone else can. We always say this and try ourselves, but know how difficult it is to achieve in practice.

Payments - Pay large sums by bank transfer whenever possible - this is also difficult in a country where cash payments, even huge amounts, are the norm. Get signed receipts. Ask for 'pink' tax slips for money transferred from the UK to your Greek bank or register the import of cash at airport control on arrival. You need these forms to prove the money was not earned in Greece (and therefore liable to tax) and to take money out of Greece when/if you sell your property.

House Insurance - Get it. Check what it includes and any conditions relating to fire cover (eg distance from fire station), security, or how long you can be away from the house. Have a full translation before committing to a Greek policy, or arrange insurance with a UK company in English.

Electrics - If you buy an old house, get modern electrical cables FROM the outside meter, not just from the fuse box. The original electrics in old village houses were probably installed just for lighting, long before they expected to use electric fires, washing machines, hair-dryers, computers, etc. *(A damaged unprotected old cable through the stone, straw and mud wall and across the dusty loft/wooden ceiling was the probable cause of our fire - it must have been perished, overloaded, or bitten by mice.)*

Advice - Don't believe the first person (official or friend) you speak to. Ask several for confirmation. Interpretation of rules varies. Don't be afraid to try people in higher office.

Building Work - Make sure you and your builder agree *exactly* what is included in the price quoted (you confirm it in writing if they won't). Often their idea of a finished job will not be yours.

Be There - Try to be present in Greece as much as possible when work is being done on your home. It can speed up the process remarkably, helps to get things the way YOU want them and minimises the risk of paying for work not done.

Value - Don't expect the value of your house to increase at the same rate as house prices in the UK and do not expect to recoup the taxes, fees and cost of renovations if you resell. If you buy a Greek home, buy it for yourself and make it how you want to enjoy it, rather than thinking of it as an investment.

Electrical Fires - Beware *update from Sue Thompson*

We had a wonderful 3 weeks at our home in Lakonia. ... The electrician wired up a new section of the house in our absence. After a couple of days there we had no electricity at all, so we got him back to sort it out. That evening after we put the water heater on we could smell burning. The fuse box got really hot. Usually we put the heater on before going to the beach for a final swim, but this evening we had friends coming so we stayed in preparing food, smelt the burning and turned the heater off.

When the electrician returned a couple of days later we saw that the metal plate the wires go through had melted in the middle and half the wires were melted together! Knowing of your problem, I daren't think what would have happened if we had gone for our normal swim.

Apart from that we only had the usual sort of mishaps, like a petrol station attendant charging €2,905 on our credit card instead of €29 !

Getting Married in Greece *by Sylvia Cook*

Getting Married in Greece, particularly somewhere that is special to you, is romantic and memorable, but the organisation and timings can be tricky to pin down. There are a number of tour companies who will organise the formalities in Greece for a civil wedding and some who can also arrange Greek Orthodox or Catholic church weddings.

For any marriage you will need:

Documents: Full Birth Certificates (inc father's name) & Certificates of No Impediment to Marriage for both parties (dated within 13 weeks of marriage date for Greek authorities) PLUS as approp: Divorce Decree Absolute, Death Certificate if widowed, Deed Poll of any name changes, PLUS current Passports.

Apart from passports, all original documents must be legalised by the UK Foreign Office, then translated to Greek by an authorised translator, then legalised by the Greek Consulate in England before presenting them in Greece.

Contacts: *(Some telephones automated so difficult to get answers)*

Local UK Registry Office (see local directory) - Visit, then Notice of Marriage posted for 21 days before issue of Certificate of No Impediment - cost £30 each (2 offices if not living in same area).

Legalisation Office, Foreign & Commonwealth Office, Old Admiralty Bldg, Whitehall, London SW1A 2LG Tel 0207 210 2521 www.fco.gov.uk/legalisation (Mon-Fri 9.30-4) - cost £12 per document to legalise. In person or allow 2-4 wks.

Consulate General of Greece, 1a Holland Park, London W11 3TP, Tel 0207 221 6467 (Mon-Fri 9.30-1) Send sae for information & list of approved translators (Arrange privately eg.£75-£100 for 4-6 docs, 2-4 wks) then £10 or £14 per document (depending on translator) for Consulate legalisation. In person or 2 wks by post. (Legalisation of documents also avail. from Birmingham Consulate - Tel 0121 454 3369)

Local Town Hall, Greece - book date in advance if you can, fees variable, documents, translations & passports required at Town Hall usually 8 days before marriage.

Try to pre-book your translator as they can get very busy at certain times.

Information correct as at 9/2002, no changes anticipated.

(More about wedding traditions & experiences in Greek-o-File Issue 2001/2)

Samos Personalities *by Ray Fordham*

Reading about Samos in an earlier issue prompted Ray Fordham to write with details of his travels there and the experiences of some of the characters he met.

Gill and I first visited Samos in 1987. At that time Samos did not figure in many brochures as there was no direct flight from the UK. We holidayed with the now defunct Intasun and stayed at the rather unfashionable north western port of Karlovassi. A short bus ride away was the very picturesque Potami Bay where we spent several enjoyable days in between sightseeing and meeting people.

Friends of ours in Plymouth, Ron and Claire, run the UK branch of a Pythagorean Society. Going back to the early 50's it was Ron's suggestion to the powers that be that the name of the birthplace of Pythagoras be changed from Tigani (the Greek word for frying pan, the shape of the harbour) to Pythagorio and the change actually took place in 1955. John Salunis had been mayor of Tigani at that time and Ron asked us to see if we could locate him in Pythagorio. After over 30 years, our first thoughts were that if he was still alive he would be rather elderly, so we were pleased when not only did we locate John - he had a gift shop on the harbour front - but he was still only in his 60's. He must have been a rather young mayor back in 1955.

Needless to say, he was delighted to meet us and invited us to his house for lunch where we met the rest of his family. John proudly showed us the Greek Journal of the time which recorded everything that had transpired with regard to the name change. Subsequently, members of the Society visited Athens and Samos in 1989 when they were entertained by their counterparts and again in 1991 when a Civic Reception was laid on.

For our second and several subsequent visits to Samos we stayed in a small Pension just behind the Harbour Front owned by a Greek gentleman

known as Mr Lambas whose life story makes fascinating reading. He joined the Greek Merchant Navy as a young lad, jumped ship twice in the States, was deported each time, but the third time he was prepared - he had paid the money for a bride! This marriage did not work out. He divorced met a Greek girl and married a second time. This did not work out either *"all she wanted was to spend my money"* - so he sent her packing.

Mr Lambas had started life in the States as a Bellboy in the Manhattan Hilton,

Mr Lambas with Ray, Gill & friend

worked his way up the ladder and ended up as Cocktail Barman with his own bar - he has photographs in his reception to prove it. Mr Lambas has another talent as a harmonica player. He told us that in his younger days he would bring the hotel kitchen to a standstill with his impromptu recitals. He was heard on one occasion by Larry Adler who was so impressed that he presented him with one of his own harmonicas.

Like most Greek immigrants, it was always the intention of Mr Lambas to return to his home island and he used to send money to his mother to finance the building of his Pension. When it was completed his employer granted him leave of absence to return to Samos for the summer months to run his Pension. Mr Lambas finally retired from the States in 1993 and returned to Samos, still single until he married a very nice lady from his home village, about 25 years younger than him.

We stayed with Mr Lambas in 1993 and one afternoon there was great excitement when the postman arrived with a letter for him from the Union awarding him a monthly pension of $188 and enclosing a cheque for the first 3 months. Although Mr Lambas spoke excellent English, like many Greeks he could not write it, so he asked us to write a letter to the Union thanking them for looking after his interests. It was duly despatched in the very next post.

Now Mr Lambas lives for most of the year in Patras where he has an apartment. He travels to Samos each summer to open his Pension. His mother who is well into her 80's also comes for the summer. We were somewhat amused to be told that just after the war mother got married for a second time to a British Soldier, Tommy from Birmingham. The marriage did not last long though as Tommy insisted on living in Birmingham and Mother refused to leave Samos.

There was another interesting old character we came across on our first visit when viewing the church adjoining the castle ruins in Pythagorio. Stelios used to delight in showing visitors around the adjoining cemetery and also showing them the 'contents' of some of the boxes in the cemetery store room.

On a subsequent visit with my son, I was intrigued to know how old he was. Stelios spoke no English so I rubbed the dust on a gravestone highlighting '87'. *"Ochi, ochi"* he said with indignation, then rubbed the dust on another gravestone - he was 85!

Our last visit to Samos was in 1996 - so it is high time we went back, hopefully to renew old acquaintances.

Stelios with Gill

From Sea Bed to Soft Sponge *by Tim Horler*

Sponges have been used by mankind since ancient times, mentioned in the Iliad around 700BC and the Bible. Who knows when someone first realised a use for their capacity to hold fluids and only release them on squeezing.

Sponges grow in oceans around the world from the Aegean and the Mediterranean, across the Atlantic to the Florida Keys, Cuba and the Caribbean and across the Pacific to Indonesia. There are many kinds but only three are commonly used. In Greece they call them Honeycomb, Silk and Elephant's ear - each name obvious when viewed. Although harvested for so long, they still need to be picked by hand and most lie beyond the range of the diver so they are not an endangered species. The main threats to their existence are from pollution and seismic activity.

Throughout history the Greeks have been at the forefront of collecting and processing sponges. In spite of the dangers of diving in deep waters, perhaps their lack of alternative income or their natural gift for marine work or the plentiful supply in the Aegean mean many Greeks are still involved in this industry today.

When sponges are collected from the sea they have a black crusty covering and they smell unpleasant. Although light in weight they look like rocks. The outer surface has a tough membrane which protects the sponge in its natural environment.

They are subjected to various processes to make them become the soft pliable sponges we would recognise. When the divers bring their harvest to the surface they first clean them of their outer crust - traditionally by stamping and walking on them with bare feet. This process also removes any 'milk' inside the pores. They are then put under tarpaulin for a while to raise the temperature and kill any organisms left in the internal canals. Next they are strung on long lines and towed behind the boat to wash away the debris before hanging them up to dry a little. Whilst still damp they are packed - very dry sponges are more brittle and easily damaged.

When the sponge vessel arrives in port merchants are invited to bid on the load. A merchant is expected to take the entire catch and will pay by the kilo. He must know where the sponges were collected and if it was an area with a muddy floor so that allowances can be made for the weight of any particles remaining in the sponges.

Sponge harvest outside town hall, laid out for merchants to view and bid

Only after purchase are they washed, sun dried and trimmed with hand shears to give them a good shape. Piles of sponge clippings cover the floor.

If anyone can think of a commercial use for the clippings, please contact me!

Trimmed sponges are immersed in acid to remove any remaining particles of shell, rock or sand and finally in a bleach solution if a lighter colour is desired. Clean, unbleached sponges are the colour of dark honey, bleached sponges vary from light honey to almost white. A good quality unbleached sponge will last 6-8 years with care, but bleaching reduces its useful life by about 25%.

The sponges are graded by size, passing them through circular holes cut in a large piece of plywood, each half an inch larger than the previous one. Graded sponges are then stored together and when sold are compressed into sacks for transport.

There are many uses for sponges today. Potters, artists, ceramic decorators and make-up artists use them commercially and in the home we use them to wash ourselves, our cars and our windows.

The Essence of Crete *by Christine Brice*

I wrote this a few years ago after spending a day riding pillion on the back of a hired Yamaha Virago motorcycle - our preferred mode of transport for exploring Greece and finding those out of the way beaches. I can still capture the essence of that holiday by rereading it - I hope you can too.

The Cretan plain spreads out in front of me
and as I ride its roads,
with the wind in my face and hair,
I can smell the history, smell the scent and the sense
of olive and vine grown for centuries.
Fresh from historical sites the land speaks to me
and voices from the past
charge the arid air with memories of past lives.
Under the burning Hellas sun
the closing of the season
and the slowing of the growing
fill the air with the pungent odour of the fruits of much labour.
The grapes, lifted sun ripe and bursting with sweetness,
lie heaped in the back of the pick-up truck and
are joyously trampled by feet eager for the fermentation
of the new year's wine to begin.
Black nets spread beneath knotty, gnarled olive trees,
like so many spiders' webs,
waiting to catch the matt black fruit to be eaten as meze
or pressed to release that golden oil
that is as vital and as radiant
as the Greek sun itself.

Greek Animal Welfare Fund Save Mr Brown

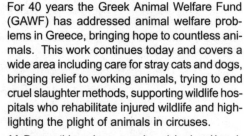

For 40 years the Greek Animal Welfare Fund (GAWF) has addressed animal welfare problems in Greece, bringing hope to countless animals. This work continues today and covers a wide area including care for stray cats and dogs, bringing relief to working animals, trying to end cruel slaughter methods, supporting wildlife hospitals who rehabilitate injured wildlife and highlighting the plight of animals in circuses.

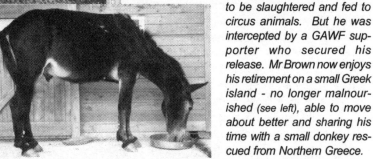

Mr Brown, this mule, was malnourished and barely able to walk. He was rounded up and on his way to be slaughtered and fed to circus animals. But he was intercepted by a GAWF supporter who secured his release. Mr Brown now enjoys his retirement on a small Greek island - no longer malnourished (see left), able to move about better and sharing his time with a small donkey rescued from Northern Greece.

Greece has few full time animal welfare workers and animal sanctuaries, so depends on a dedicated network of volunteers throughout the country including volunteer vets on working holidays who help with neutering cats and dogs and attending to sick animals.

The GAWF biannual magazine 'Elpida' (meaning *Hope*) gives many examples of their work and keeps members up to date with their activities, including currently a programme to educate young Greeks about animal welfare.

Another article in the last Elpida highlights the plight of working donkeys in Santorini, hired out to save tourists the walk up to town. Although generally in good body condition, there were several with scars from tethering and there seemed no evidence of the animals being fed during the working day from 8am to 7-8pm. Think about this next time you contemplate the 'easy' ride to the top. YOU have a choice. Have you been fed and watered?

If you would like to know more and to help GAWF in their work, you can become a member for £15 annually, or just send a donation to :
Greek Animal Welfare Fund, 1-2 Castle Lane, London SW1E 6DN
Telephone 020 7828 9736, email admin@gawf.freeserve.co.uk

Greece: Land of Wild Flowers *by John Akeroyd*

Botanist and contributor on several occasions, Dr John Akeroyd tells us about the wild flowers of Greece, a never to be forgotten spectacle for many spring visitors.

Greece is both a land of antiquities and a land of flowers. Few visitors in late winter and spring, when the countryside wears its mantle of fresh green, can fail to notice the masses of wild flowers. They add interest and colour to roadsides, pastures, fields and olive groves, and beaches, cliffs and rocky ground. Up to 40 or so years ago visitors would also comment on the wild flowers on and around archaeological sites. Indeed for years organised botanical tours to Greece were based on a successful 'Sites and Flowers' formula – but few flowers remain there today as the custodians liberally spray the smallest green shoot with herbicides. Farmers too have tended to over-spray in recent years and suburban sprawl has done much damage to coastal habitats.

However, the flora remains substantially intact. And one or two archaeological sites, notably Mystra near Sparta (spurges, honesty, anemones and bellflowers) remain natural rock gardens. Botanists have identified a remarkable total of some 5000 species of wild flower (including trees and

shrubs) in Greece, giving this small country one of Europe's and Earth's richest floras. Turkey has twice that number of species but is a huge country. Greece is as rich in flowers as Spain, another large country that also takes in the Balearic and Canary Islands. The Greek flora compares well with those of many small tropical countries and is larger than those of most countries in the arid Tropics. In Europe only Italy has more species, but does include Sardinia, Sicily and a large portion of the Alps!

So, why does Greece have so many wild flowers? The reasons are several, all happy accidents of time and geography. First, Greece sits at a crossroads between Europe and Asia, a natural

Turban Buttercups - can occur in thousands

meeting point for plant migration routes over millennia. Second, it is a topographically dissected landscape of islands, peninsulas and mountains, which has cut off and isolated populations of plants and thus created suitable conditions for evolutionary divergence (like Darwin's famous finches in the Galapagos Islands). After the Ice Ages, when plant species retreated south, many remained in suitable habitats in the Balkan Peninsula and never migrated north. Heather-like Bruckenthalia is now found only in the mountains of northern Greece and the Balkans, yet we have fossil evidence for its existence in Britain before the last Ice Age! Geology too has played its part, with large areas of limestone and some special plants restricted to serpentine in the Pindhos Mountains and elsewhere.

The flowers themselves are a varied assemblage. Some are familiar wayside plants from home, others are Turkish or African plants at the edge of their range. Many, especially the spiny ones, are widespread Mediterranean species and at least a third are specialities of Greece and the adjacent region, the so-called endemics.

Buckler Mustard

A few larger plant families dominate the spring flora. The cress family, with often pungent leaves and always four petals appropriately arranged as a Greek cross, provides much of the bulk:- wild cabbages, rockets, mustards, shepherd's purse and honesty. So does the clover family – countless clovers, trefoils, medicks, vetches and, on Crete, purplish-pink Giant Sainfoin. The daisy and dandelion family, with broad heads of massed tiny florets, is responsible for much of the ubiquitous yellow colours: Crown Daisy, in yellow or white-and-yellow dominates huge areas in late spring, and Salsify dots grassy places with lilac. The carrot family adds architecture, especially the huge yellow fennels and the delicate white Tordylium, with elegant piecrust-edged fruits. The aromatic mint family gives much of the characteristic scent to the Greek

Wild Radish

landscape: a host of wild culinary herbs such as sages, thymes, savories, lavenders, rosemary (usually about villages), as well as the striking yellow-flowered Jerusalem Sage. Two other families, the mostly blue borages and the scarlet poppies add variety to a mix that is sometimes a bit heavy on yellows!

And, of course, another huge family is the orchids – ever-popular and one that lends a touch of the truly exotic to spring hillsides. The flowers, usually in spikes or clusters, come in all shapes and colours, each with a central lip, smaller side-petals and often a long spur. Robust, early-flowering Giant orchid and the pink-flowered Naked Man Orchid and Pyramidal Orchid are common enough; some others are rare and none should ever be picked. The most exciting are the bee-orchids or *Ophrys* that have a lip shaped like a small furry insect. The flower mimics a female bee or wasp, even exuding a similar scent, so as to attract a male insect that pollinates the orchid's flower whilst he attempts to mate with it. Some species such as Yellow Bee-orchid and Late Spider-orchid are widespread, even locally abundant.

Late Spider-orchid, one of many bee orchids

Caper

Even in the lowlands some flowers bloom all through the summer. The caper is a good example, seen hanging in tangled masses from walls, especially old fortifications, and from seaside rocks and cliffs. It is an ancient tropical relic in the Mediterranean whose nearest relatives occur in the warmer parts of Africa and Asia. The capers we see pickled in jars are the young buds of this plant, not the fruits.

Cretan Tulip, found only on Crete in rocks & stony fields

Bulbs are an attractive group, mostly members of the lily and iris families. These tend to flower early, often in winter, and many visitors miss the best of them. In February, even hillsides close to Athens can be covered with pale mauve crocus and tiny blue grape hyacinths; damp ground near the sea can be a mass of narcissus. One of my favourite displays was yellow crocus-like Sternbergia on rocks near the Acropolis on a sunny November afternoon. These out-of-season displays often involve dodging cold winds and showers! Fortunately some attractive bulbs flower at holiday times; White and Yellow Asphodel stand erect like sentinels in springtime, and metre-tall Giant Squill (flowering without leaves) adds life to parched landscapes from early September. In high summer, the magnificent fragrant white-flowered Sea Daffodil blooms even on some tourist beaches.

The traveller to Greece who penetrates inland and up into the hills and mountains (even in the islands) will discover the richest floral displays of all. Here flowers last well into and sometimes through the summer. In fact, the majority of Greek wild flowers bloom in June and July – but mostly in the mountains. To see them at their best one needs to take stout boots and provisions and explore *'me ta podia'*. It is worth the effort to see high rocky grassland covered in flowers; or search out choice endemics on cliffs and screes. Several mountains now have good forest roads, paths and mountain hut accommodation. Mount Olympos is easy to climb (if a slog!) and has more flowers than the whole British Isles, including 25 unique endemics.

Back in the lowlands, another burst of colour from September to November signals the arrival of autumn and winter bulbs. Go to the Mani in November - you will never forget the sheets of colchicum, crocus, daffodils and squills.

Greek Food & Cooking

Greek Fast Food *by Sylvia Cook*

Illustrations by Gill Tomlinson

When we speak of 'fast food' in most countries it means American style burgers, seasoned over-battered chicken, or pizzas. Whilst burger bars and pizzas are certainly to be found in Greece, for the best value and for the flavour of Greece we recommend you try 'real' Greek fast food.

In any Greek town and many villages you will find small souvlaki bars and Greek pie shops offering takeaway or eat in food probably cheaper than you could cook it for yourself.

Gyros Pitta - our favourite. Forget those Turkish or Cypriot donner kebabs where you are unsure how long the minced meat mass has been going round and round, with the grill turned on then off; also forget those hard pitta bread pockets. In Greece they pile pieces of pork, usually good lean meat, on to the central skewer which 'gyrates' (γύρος - a Greek word of course) in front of the grill. It sells like hot cakes so is always fresh. Chunks of delicious tasty meat cooked in its own juices are sliced off and loaded onto a round soft pancake pitta (more like a fried naan bread). Slices of tomato,

onion and other salad, a dollop of tsatsiki, sometimes cool mustard sauce, and finally a few chips are loaded in before it is rolled up in greaseproof paper and wrapped with a serviette ready to eat. It is a meal in itself.

Other Pittas - More and more often in recent years we've also had **chicken** gyros as an option made the same way as above, or local **sausage** pitta, or **bifteki** (μπιφτέκι) pitta with a small home-made herbed hamburger fried on the hot griddle. Perhaps you have tried bifteki before with a plated meal. Or they usually have **souvlaki pittas** - a skewer (kamaki) of small pork cubes (occasionally other meats) cooked quickly on the griddle instead of the gyros meat. Portions and prices vary tremendously, but even if they are not so generous and you feel you want a second one, it is a very cheap meal washed down with a beer or village wine.

They will usually ask if you want *'olla mesa'* (all inside), so if you don't like any of the contents they can be left out. If you prefer **plain meat** you can order a number of souvlakia sticks which will be served with a piece of bread, or a 'plate' of the gyros meat, or priced by weight - or they will fill a foil container with succulent tasty gyros meat to take away.

Most souvlaki bars have a few chairs and tables where you can sit down to eat and perhaps a wider menu including salads, chips and the tastiest rotisserie grilled chicken or even lamb.

Cheese Pies - The hand pulled barrow full of hot cheese pies (tiropitta / τυρόπιτα) is a familiar morning sight in many Greek shopping areas in towns and bigger villages. The cheese (usually feta) is wrapped in flaky or filo pastry, kept warm and served in a greaseproof packet. Just the thing to fill a hole in your stomach if you've got up early to go to the town. The pastry can be a bit messy though, leaving crumbs all over your clothes and hands.

Better still, if there is a hot pie shop with circular coiled cheese rolls or large rectangular pies cut into portions in a heated window display, you may be able to sit down at the counter or in a corner and enjoy your breakfast or lunch pie with a cup of refreshing coffee or a cold drink. Generally there is a choice of cheese (τυρόπιτα), or spinach (σπανακόπιτα) or **cheese and spinach pies**. The large coils are sold by the portion and are usually very generous - cut into 3-4 cm lengths and piled into an open foil lined box, with a plastic fork to feed yourself (and keep the oil and pastry off your hands). One portion is usually enough for us to share between two.

If you are able to spend more time in Greece, but can't afford to eat out at tavernas all the time, these Greek fast-food shops are a convenient, more sociable and enjoyable way of eating than cooking in your studio or home and need not cost any more. Using local ingredients the food on offer has an unmistakable Greek flavour and the small establishments offer the usual Greek friendly welcome.

Don't let the Greeks keep this part of their lifestyle to themselves. Go and join them. They won't mind at all.

Tirosalata Kafteri / Spicy Cheese Dip *by Sylvia Cook*

Don't you just love the Greek way of having a little nibble of something when you have a beer or ouzo - not a meal, just something to fill a space and keep you going until later. We often order a plate with a selection (*pikilia*) of dips and some bread for a snack with a beer or glass of wine after a late afternoon on the beach as the sun slips down. It's one of those things that isn't on the menu where we go, but our friend is always happy to oblige.

This is one of the favourites we ask to be included if he has it. Kostas explained it was just creamed feta cheese with pepper, so I tried it as simply as that with black pepper and it was tasty, but back in UK I checked out my Greek recipe books and discovered he meant chilli pepper which tastes far better. Apparently it is a speciality of Macedonia - where Kostas is from.

With a little more experimentation I came up with the following:

> *200 gr Greek feta cheese (you could also use soft mizithra)*
>
> *1 long red chilli pepper, fresh (or chilli sauce or tabasco to taste)*
>
> *3-4 tablespoons olive oil*

Method

☐ Grill the red chilli pepper to blacken, or hold over a gas flame skewered on stick, turning to blacken all the skin. Cool a little, then remove the skin and seeds and cut flesh into very small pieces. Be careful to wash hands thoroughly after preparing the chilli as the pepper juice can harm eyes, lips or other delicate areas.

☐ Mash the feta cheese with a fork. Combine with chilli and olive oil with a pestle and mortar or electric blender until the consistency of a paste.

☐ Sprinkle the top with a touch of paprika and serve with chunks of bread and/or raw vegetables (eg carrots, celery).

(If you can't get hold of fresh chilli peppers, it is simple to make and tastes pretty good just substituting a splash of tabasco or hot chilli sauce.)

Courgette & Cheese Bake *by Sylvia Cook*

Lighter than a pastry base pie, more easily made and less calories than courgette fritters, this recipe can be used for a vegetarian dish, a starter or meze dish, or cut in fingers for a buffet meal or party dish.

1 kilo courgettes

3 eggs

3 tablespoons single cream

200 gr yellow cheese (kaseri, gruyere, cheddar, double gloucester)

2 tablespoons olive oil

3 tablespoons flour

oregano, salt & pepper

Method

☐ Grate courgettes and salt lightly. Leave in colander with a plate on top. Drain at least 1 hour.

☐ Preheat oven, Gas Mark 6 / 200°C.

☐ Mix together the beaten eggs, cream, oil, grated cheese, flour, oregano and black pepper. Squeeze excess water from the courgettes by hand and stir into the mixture.

☐ Butter a deep baking tray or large rectangular casserole dish and spread courgette mixture evenly.

☐ Place in hot oven and bake 40-50 minutes, or until golden brown. (If reducing quantities for a smaller bake, it takes less time).

☐ Remove from oven. Leave to cool a little before cutting into wedges, fingers or squares to suit serving requirements. (Can be cooked in advance and warmed through to serve.)

Marinated Roast or Barbecued Lamb - *by Janet Ellis*

The first time Janet and husband Peter ate this was at the Eros Greek Restaurant in Henley on Thames (sadly now an Italian restaurant). It was the chef's own *unique* version of **Kleftiko**, which he kindly divulged. It may not be the traditional 'bandits' cooking method, but they first tasted this before visiting Greece, so to them it will always be *'kleftiko'* and a firm favourite.

Janet has adapted the recipe from oven cooking for BBQ cooking too.

> *Half leg of fresh lamb, fillet end (or half shoulder oven method only)*
> *1 tablsp each of dried thyme, oregano, rosemary, Hungarian paprika*
> *2 onions thickly sliced, 2 cups olive oil*

Oven Method

❑ Start about Monday to be ready for cooking Friday or Saturday. Make large slashes with a sharp knife across the surface of the lamb. Place in a large dish and cover with dried herbs, onions and copious quantities of olive oil. I don't measure, so the above quantities are a guideline.

❑ Rub the marinade well into the meat, cover dish and place in the fridge, turning every 12 hours, until you are ready to cook it.

❑ Preheat oven to Gas Mark 4 / 180°C. Put lamb and marinade with roughly chopped potatoes <u>uncovered</u> in oven for about 1½ hours. Baste the lamb and potatoes regularly throughout the cooking period. When it is cooked to taste remove to a warm plate. Leave it to rest for about ½ hour. Cut meat into thick slices and serve with the potatoes and onions.

❑ We enjoy this with flat beans, tomatoes and onions (all home grown in season) cooked in olive oil, or, if you omit the potatoes, with spinach cooked with rice and dill and, of course, a good bottle of Greek wine.

Barbecue Method

❑ Marinate the meat for just 48 hours in the warmer months, using ½ leg of lamb (fillet end), boned and split open first. (Shoulder is too smoky on the BBQ from the fat melting and dripping onto the coals).

❑ Husband Peter (our BBQ supremo) takes over at this point and cooks the lamb slowly well above the coals, turning frequently and brushing with excess marinade each turn, for about 45 mins, depending on the heat of the coals and the thickness of the lamb. Again leave the lamb ½ hour. While it is resting cook the marinade onions in some of the excess herbed marinade oil in a pan on the top of the BBQ.

❑ In the summer this goes well with a crisp lettuce salad with red onions and fennel, tossed in olive oil and a little sea salt, topped with Thassos olives (courtesy of our friends there), some home-made bread (try feta and mint) to mop up the meat juices and a bottle of chilled retsina.

Yiouvetsi by Sylvia Cook

Yiouvetsi (Γιουβέτσι) is an oven baked dish made with lamb or beef, characterised by the addition of rice shaped pasta, called *manestra* in Greece. You can buy the pasta in Mediterranean specialist shops in UK, or bring it back from the local supermarket as a useful holiday souvenir. It is often prepared in individual earthenware dishes, or just one large earthenware casserole.

to Serve 4 :

750-800 gr lean braising beef or leg of lamb

1 cup manestra pasta (macaroni or other pasta if not available)

1 standard tin tomatoes (or 1 lb fleshy ripe tomatoes)

1 onion chopped

2 tablespoons olive oil

2 cloves garlic (optional)

salt and black pepper

100 gr kaseri or cheddar cheese

Method

☐ Preheat oven Gas mark 4 / 180°C.

☐ Cut meat into small pieces. Place in earthenware oven dish or 4 small dishes. Roughly chop tomatoes (peel and chop, add 1 cup water if using fresh tomatoes). Mix with chopped onion, crushed garlic, olive oil and seasoning. Add to meat, equally divided if using small dishes.

☐ Cover, place in oven and bake about 2 hours until meat is tender. If using small uncovered dishes you will need to check from time to time to ensure they do not dry out. (You may prefer to casserole all the meat together up to this stage and then share out into smaller dishes).

☐ Add 2 cups of hot water and the pasta to the dishes and return to oven uncovered for a further 40 minutes, by which time the liquid should all be absorbed into the pasta which remains moist. (Check whilst cooking and top up with more hot water if absorbing the liquid too soon.)

☐ Grate the cheese and sprinkle over the dishes. Return to the oven to melt - about 5 minutes - before serving.

The pasta tastes delicious, having absorbed the tomato and meat juices and the meat should be beautifully tender from slow braising. Serve on its own or with a side salad or green vegetables.

Baklava *by Margy Gulland*

Margy says "My recipe for baklava is very simple. It always seems to turn out OK even though I vary the quantities slightly."

250g filo pastry	**For syrup :**
125g butter	100g sugar
20g breadcrumbs	65 ml water
50g castor sugar	1 tablespoon lemon juice
250g walnuts, chopped	65 ml honey
1 teaspoon cinnamon	¼ teaspoon vanilla essence
(optional) pinch of powdered cloves	

Method

☐ Mix breadcrumbs, sugar, walnuts and cinnamon together.

☐ Preheat oven to Gas Mark 4 / 180°C electric. Melt butter in small pan, remove from heat.

☐ Unwrap filo pastry. Count how many sheets you have (it varies). Cut through the middle of the sheets, all together, making pieces a bit bigger than your baking tin/dish. Put all filo in one pile, loosely cover with a tea towel to keep from drying out while you are not using it.

☐ Using a pastry brush, lightly butter the base of a rectangular oven dish (8" x 10"). Butter the top of the first filo sheet generously and place in dish. Fold edges in to fit. Continue 1 sheet at a time until about ⅕ of the filo sheets have been added, brushing the top of each with butter.

☐ Sprinkle ¼ walnut mixture evenly over the filo in the pan.

☐ Butter and add another ⅕ of the filo sheets in layers, then another ¼ of the walnut mixture. Continue until all the mixture is used up, ending with a filo layer. Using a sharp knife, cut through the top layers only to mark into pieces. Pour any remaining butter over the top. Bake in the oven for 45-60 minutes until golden.

☐ 15 mins before you expect to take it out of the oven, make the syrup. Put water, sugar and lemon juice in pan and cook over medium heat until it goes slightly syrupy and very pale yellow (about 10-15 mins.).

☐ Remove from heat, add honey and vanilla, stir until well blended. If you like your baklava very sticky you can increase the amount of syrup.

☐ Remove the baklava from oven and pour the hot syrup over the top.

☐ Cool, cover and leave for at least 48 hours before eating.

The longer you leave it the better it gets!

Retsina - The Wine Taste of Greece *by Sylvia Cook*

The Greeks have been producing wines for about 4,000 years. With many excellent indigenous grape varieties and a perfect vine growing climate they are now making and exporting many wines of outstanding quality.

However, for many, it is the acquired taste of the unusual resin flavoured wines that most easily recreates memories of Greece. Fortunately such wines are available at budget prices, so a Greek meal can be recreated at home with a bottle of retsina to really put you in the Greek mood.

Origin of Retsina - The Greeks knew in ancient times that air was the enemy of wine, so they sealed their wine jars with resin from the pine tree. As a further precaution they added resin to the wine itself to form a protective film between it and the air. This kept the air out of the grape must and ensured the wine did not oxidise. They found it kept much longer and soon got used to the resinous flavour imparted to the wines. I also heard that they continued resinating their wines because their Turkish oppressors (and other invaders over the centuries) did not like the flavour, so their supplies would not be plundered.

Retsina Today - Now winemaking methods are more effective at keeping air from contaminating wines. However, once acquired, the taste of retsina is enjoyed by many. It is a particularly pleasant wine for supping well chilled with a few mezedes, or with fried or spicy foods. Today's producers add resin from the conifer 'Pinus Halepensis' to give the wine that distinctive flavour to a greater or lesser extent. Most retsinas are made from the savatiano grape, the most widespread variety in Greece today.

Many wine buffs are snobbish about retsina, but there are a number available which have a consistent flavour and are good value for money. I was pleased to see several retsinas included in Geoff Adams' Greek Wines - A Comprehensive Guide (reviews).

In Greece you will usually find a retsina barrel wine option in tavernas where wine is sold by the carafe (or kilo). You will also find retsina bottled in 500ml clear bottles the shape of beer bottles and VERY reasonably priced in super-markets or some traditional tavernas. It is also available in standard size, 1 and 1½ litre bottles - a real Greek party wine!

The biggest selling bottled retsina in both Greece and UK is Kourtakis with its distinctive yellow label. It is available from most of the large supermarket chains in UK. They also have a 500ml beer bottle size available in Greece.

There are a number of wineries making the half litre bottles sold in Greece. We decided to bring a few back to conduct a mini tasting experiment with friends in Britain.

We had to have a **Kourtaki Retsina** of course. It's the one everyone knows so a useful comparison if you are not ac-customed to describing the taste of a wine. The agreed opinion was that it was consistent, quaffable, fairly light with a fresh taste of resin. Comparing with a standard bottle we decided we could not taste a difference although in Greece we had imagined we could!

The **Malamatina** was a lighter colour and had 'a flowery nose in a retsina kind of way' someone said. It had a much lighter taste and a citrusy sharpness. The resin taste was less obvious.

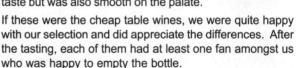

The **Marko** Retsina Markopoulou had a richer colour and a much stronger resin taste but was also smooth on the palate.

If these were the cheap table wines, we were quite happy with our selection and did appreciate the differences. After the tasting, each of them had at least one fan amongst us who was happy to empty the bottle.

By contrast (not wasted on the above session) we were given a 'good' bottle of retsina, a **Ritinitis Noblis** produced by the **Gaia** estate which had been recommended by a wine expert who felt most retsinas weren't worth touching. It was in a tall slim green (posh) bottle, and was obviously a better quality wine with more interesting flavour, but very little resin taste and very light. It is, unusually for retsina, made from the roditis grape. Perhaps those who think

they don't like retsina would appreciate the lighter resin taste of Ritinitis Noblis. Interestingly in Geoff Adams book he rates it the same as the Kourtakis at 6/10 - high quality, very interesting and very pleasant.

Eating Greek in the UK

Recommended UK Greek & Cypriot Restaurants & Tavernas

There are many Greek & Cypriot restaurants in UK and others where a range of Mediterranean or other cuisine is also on offer. Few offer food quite like 'mamma's cooking' in our favourite holiday taverna, but they do give us a taste of those lazy days, sunshine and good times to remind us of Greece when we can't be there.

We asked Greek-o-File subscribers to tell us about their favourites. Due to limited space, we have omitted some with just one recommendation in areas well provided for, but in areas less well served we have tried to include at least one. Several told us, *sadly none in our area!'* Let us know if you can fill in some gaps. (Arranged by region (N to S), number of recommendations in brackets).

SCOTLAND

Christos Greek Taverna (6) *
14-20 John Street, ABERDEEN
Grampian AB25 1BT
Tel: 01224 636320

Santorini (2)
32c Broughton Street, EDINBURGH
Lothian EH1 3SB
Tel: 0131 557 2012

Konaki Restaurant (2)
920 Sauchiehall Street, GLASGOW
Strathclyde G3 7TF
Tel: 0141 342 4010

Parthenon Greek Restaurant (3)
725 Great Western Road
GLASGOW, Strathclyde G12 8QX
Tel: 0141 334 6265

The Greek Kebab Restaurant (3)
34 Sinclair Drive, off Battlefield Road
GLASGOW, Strathclyde G42 9QE
Tel: 0141 649 7581

Aris Greek Restaurant (1)
55 Eastwoodmains Road, Williamwood
GLASGOW, Strathclyde G46 6PW
Tel: 0141 638 8422

Cafe Serghei (3)
67 Bridge Street, GLASGOW
Strathclyde G5 9JB
Tel: 0141 429 1547

NORTH WEST

Alexandros Restaurant (3)
68 Warwick Road, CARLISLE
Cumbria CA1 1DR
Tel: 01228 592227

BOUZOUKI BY NIGHT (3)
88 Princess Street
MANCHESTER M1 6NG
Tel: 0161 236 9282

SOKRATES GREEK TAVERNA (6) *
80 Winterhay Road, Horwich
BOLTON, Grt Manchester BL6 7NZ
Tel: 01204 692100

SOKRATES GREEK TAVERNA (1)
25a Northenden Road, SALE, Cheshire
M33 2DL **Tel: 0161 282 0050**

Traditional Greek & Cypriot food.
Live Greek music & dancing at
Bouzouki by Night *for large & small parties. Sokrates Tavernas some events.*
Owner - Photis Nasaris

Kosmos Taverna Restaurant (6) *
248 Wilmslow Road
MANCHESTER M14 9NF
Tel: 0161 225 9106

Zorba's Kebab House (3)
279 Barlow Moor Road, Chorlton
MANCHESTER M21 7GH
Tel: 0161 881 7750

The Original Greek Restaurant (3)
35-37 Church Street, COLNE
Lancashire BB8 0EB
Tel: 01282 859500

Giggi's Taverna (6) *
21a Church Street, BLACKPOOL
Lancashire FY1 4RP
Tel: 01253 622936

The Cafe Neon Greek Taverna (5) *
3 Clifton Street, LYTHAM
Lancashire FY8 5EP
Tel: 01253 737979

DIONYSUS Greek Taverna (4)*

1 Rochdale Road East
HEYWOOD, Lancs OL10 4DX
Tel: 01706 691444
(Estd. 1998)

Traditional Greek Food
Authentic atmosphere

Limassol Taverna (3)
17 Baldwin Street, ST HELENS
Merseyside WA10 2RS
Tel: 01744 453273

Lazaros Greek Taverna (6) *
49 Market Street, Hoylake, WIRRAL
Merseyside CH47 2BQ
Tel: 0151 632 0400

Phylachae's Greek Taverna (2)
32-34 Bromborough Village Rd
Bromborough, WIRRAL
Merseyside CH62 7ET
Tel: 0151 334 8437

Artemis Restaurant (1)
117-119 South Road, WATERLOO
Merseyside L22 0LR
Tel: 0151 476 6046

Christakis Greek Taverna (2)
7 York Street (off Duke Street)
LIVERPOOL, Merseyside L1 5BN
Tel: 0151 708 7377

The Kebab House (3)
22 Hardman Street, LIVERPOOL
Merseyside L1 9AX
Tel: 0151 709 4885

Lefteris Restaurant (2)
63 Allerton Road, LIVERPOOL
Merseyside L18 2DA
Tel: 0151 475 5777

Aphrodite Restaurant (1)
15 High Park Place, Churchtown
SOUTHPORT, Merseyside PR9 7QP
Tel: 01704 232214

NORTH EAST

Costa's Restaurant (2)
1st Floor, 84 Princes Avenue, HULL
Humberside HU5 3QL
Tel: 01482 445018

The Greek Taverna (1)
224 Beverley Road, HULL, HU5 1AH
Tel: 01482 447989

Mana Greek Restaurant (3)
10 St Sampsons Square, YORK
North Yorkshire YO1 8RN
Tel: 01904 627793

Aphrodite Greek Restaurant
4 Brockwell Centre, Northumbrian Road
CRAMLINGTON, Northumb. NE23 1XZ
Tel: 01670 736070

The Mad Greek
117 Fitzwilliam Street, SHEFFIELD
South Yorkshire S1 4JP
Tel: 0114 272 6000

Cafe Neon (2)
8 Bigg Market, NEWCASTLE-UPON-
TYNE, Tyne & Wear NE1 1UW
Tel: 0191 260 2577

Simply Greek (3)
6 Bigg Market, NEWCASTLE-UPON-
TYNE, Tyne & Wear NE1 1UW
Tel: 0191 232 0750

Theo's Restaurant (3)
12-16 Bridgegate, HEBDEN BRIDGE
West Yorkshire HX7 8EX
Tel: 01422 845337

La Tavas (1)
229 Kings Cross Road, HALIFAX
West Yorkshire HX1 3JL
Tel: 01422 364747

Artemis Restaurant (3)
8b - 10b Market Street Arcade, LEEDS
West Yorkshire LS1 6DH
Tel: 0113 243 3737

The Olive Tree (4) *
Oaklands, 55 Rodley Lane, LEEDS
West Yorkshire LS13 1NG
Tel: 0113 256 9283

WALES

Greek Taverna (1)
12-14 Holyhead Road, BANGOR
Gwynedd LL57 2EG
Tel: 01248 354991

The Aegean Taverna (2)
117 Woodville Road, Cathays, CARDIFF
South Glamorgan CF24 4DY
Tel: 0292 034 5114

Aphrodite (1)
8-12 Crwys Road, Roath, CARDIFF
South Glamorgan CF2 4NS
Tel: 0292 045 6914

CENTRAL

Acropolis (1)
36 St Peters Street, BEDFORD
Bedfordshire MK40 2NN
Tel: 01234 341798 / 341780

Steliana's & Sapho's Greek Taverna (3)
7 Old Blacksmiths Yard, Saddler Gate
DERBY, Derbyshire DE1 3PD
Tel: 01332 385200

Troodos Taverna (1)
99 Dominion Road, GLENFIELD
Leicestershire LE3 8JB
Tel: 0116 287 3732

Pappas Greek Restaurant (1)
25 Radcliffe Road, West Bridgeford
NOTTINGHAM, Notts NG2 5FF
Tel: 0115 981 9091

Pauncefote Arms (1)
Fosse Road, East Stoke, NEWARK
Nottinghamshire NG23 5QQ
Tel: 01636 525226
*Greek food always on the menu at this
village bar & restaurant, PLUS special
Greek Nights with dancing display &
participation. **B&B** too!*

The Greek Restaurant (2)
79-80 Bolebridge Street, TAMWORTH
Staffordshire B79 7PD
Tel: 01827 316506

Athenia Greek Restaurant (2)
49 Corporation Street, COVENTRY
Warwickshire CV1 1GH
Tel: 02476 63 4949

Tarsus Restaurant (2)
Daventry Road (A425), Southam,
LEAMINGTON SPA, Warks. CV47 1NW
Tel: 01926 813585

Athens Greek Restaurant (2)
30/31 Paradise Circus, BIRMINGHAM
West Midlands B1 2BJ
Tel: 0121 643 5523

Zorba's Greek Restaurant (2)
359-361 Olton Boulevard East,
Acocks Green, BIRMINGHAM B27 7DP
Tel: 0121 706 4709

Zorba's Greek Restaurant (3)
624 Washwood Heath Road, Ward End
BIRMINGHAM, West Midlands B8 2HG
Tel: 0121 327 5554

Souvlaki Greek Taverna (2)
50 Friar Street, WORCESTER
Worcestershire WR1 2NA
Tel: 01905 22972

Azure Mediterranean Restaurant (2)
33-35 Broad Street, WORCESTER
Worcestershire WR1 5NT
Tel: 01905 25832

EAST

Varsity Restaurant (1)
35 St Andrew Street, CAMBRIDGE
Cambridgeshire CB2 3AR
Tel: 01223 356060

Bella Pais (1)
7 Centurian House
St John's Street, COLCHESTER
Essex CO2 7AH
Tel: 01206 571830

Meze Meze (2)
376-378 Cranbrook Road, Gants Hill
ILFORD, Essex IG2 6HW
Tel: 020 8554 1121

Corinthian Taverna (1)
391 Eastern Avenue, Gants Hill
ILFORD, Essex IG2 6LR
Tel: 020 8554 2060

Pisces Greek Taverna (2)
25 The Broadway, WICKFORD
Essex SS11 7AD
Tel: 01268 732001

Mylos Taverna (1)
376 High Street, LINCOLN,
Lincolnshire LN5 7RY
Tel: 01522 575550

Othello Restaurant (1)
23 Bethlehem Street, GRIMSBY
Lincolnshire DN31 1JN
Tel: 01472 356704

© The Greek-o-File™ Vol. I

Page 127

Krasades Taverna (4) *
17 Prince of Wales Road, NORWICH
Norfolk NR1 1BD
Tel: 016 0361 6791

Constantia Cottage Restaurant (3)
East Runton, CROMER
Norfolk NR27 9NX
Tel: 01263 512017

Othello Restaurant (1)
55 Marine Parade, GREAT
YARMOUTH, Norfolk NR30 2EJ
Tel: 01493 843825

The Greek Taverna (1)
22b Hatter Street, BURY ST
EDMUNDS, Suffolk IP33 1NE
Tel: 01284 752900/ 703717

SOUTH WEST

The Kebab House (2)
6 St Michaels Hill, BRISTOL
Avon BS2 8DT
Tel: 0117 921 1958

Grecian Kebab House (1)
2 Cromwell Road, St Andrews
BRISTOL, Avon BS6 5AA
Tel: 0117 942 3456

Dimitris Taverna (1)
18 Richmond Street, WESTON-
SUPER-MARE Avon BS23 1SY
Tel: 01934 620187

Marine Bar & Restaurant (1)
Falmouth Yacht Marina, North Parade
FALMOUTH, Cornwall TR11 2DT
Tel: 01326 313481

Lanterns Kebab & Steak House (2)
88 Cornwall Street, PLYMOUTH
Devon PL1 1LR
Tel: 01752 665516

The Village Restaurant (3)
31a Southside Street, The Barbican
PLYMOUTH, Devon PL1 2LE
Tel: 01752 667688

The Vines Taverna (1)
43 Fore Street, IVYBRIDGE
Devon PL21 9AE
Tel: 01752 895007

Romanzo Greek Taverna (2)
87 Poole Road, BOURNEMOUTH
Dorset BH4 9BB
Tel: 01202 761070

SOUTH CENTRAL

Latino Greek Restaurant (3)
3 Church Lane, WINDSOR
Berks SL4 1PA
Tel: 01753 857711

Santorini Greek Restaurant (2)
Hazlemere Crossroads, Hazlemere
HIGH WYCOMBE, Bucks HP15 7LG
Tel: 01494 714999

Alexiou's Taverna (1)
High Street, CHIPPING CAMPDEN
Gloucestershire GL55 6AG
Tel: 01386 840826

Athens Greek Taverna (1)
Salem House, Clarence Parade
CHELTENHAM Glos. GL50 3PA
Tel: 01242 237200

Elias Restaurant (1)
79 Canal Walk, SOUTHAMPTON
Hants SO14 3BH
Tel: 023 8022 2699

Aphrodite Kebab House (1)
39 Long Lane, Holbury
SOUTHAMPTON Hants SO45 2LG
Tel: 02380 891805

Kyriakos Greek Restaurant (1)
30 Holywell Hill,
ST ALBANS, Herts AL1 1BZ
Tel: 01727 832841 / 838977

Parthenon Restaurant (1)
6a Adelaide Street, ST ALBANS
Herts AL3 5BH
Tel:01727 846152

The Coach House Taverna (1)
London Road, Langley
HITCHIN, Herts SG4 7PP
Tel: 01438 821054

The Green Olive (1)
28 Market Place, HENLEY ON
THAMES, Oxon RG9 2AH
Tel: 01491 412220

The Greek Taverna
272 Banbury Road, OXFORD OX2 7DY
Tel: 01865 511472

LONDON

The Real Greek (3)
14-15 Hoxton Market, Shoreditch
LONDON N1 6HG
Tel: 020 7739 8212

Fanari Greek Restaurant (2)
62 Alderman's Hill, Palmers Green
LONDON N13 4PP
Tel: 020 8882 8085 / 4

Vrisaki Kebab House (2)
73 Myddleton Road, Wood Green
LONDON N22 4LZ
Tel: 020 8889 8760 / 020 8881 2920

Lemonia Greek Restaurant (2)
89 Regents Park Road, Primrose Hill
LONDON NW1 8UY
Tel: 020 7586 7454

Limani Restaurant (1)
154 Regents Park Road,
LONDON NW13XN
Tel: 020 7483 4492

Cafe Corfu (3)
7-9 Pratt Street, Camden
LONDON NW1 0AE
Tel: 020 7267 8088

D & G Kebab House (1)
2 Station Parade, Walm Lane
LONDON NW2 4NH
Tel: 020 8450 6166

Halepi Restaurant (1)
48-50 Belsize Lane
LONDON NW3 5AR
Tel: 020 7431 5855

Mario's Restaurant (1)
153 Broadhurst Gardens, West
Hampstead, LONDON NW6 3QR
Tel: 020 7625 5827

Aphrodite Greek Restaurant (1)
19 Westow Street, Crystal Palace
LONDON SE19 3RY
Tel: 020 8653 9895

The Village Taverna (1)
116 Lee Road, Blackheath
LONDON SE3 9DE
Tel: 020 8318 9462

Nico's Acropolis Taverna (2)
396 Footscray Road, New Eltham
LONDON SE9 3TU
Tel: 020 8850 9696

Oracle Restaurant (1)
263 Putney Bridge Road, Putney
LONDON SW15 2PU
Tel: 020 8780 1585 / 020 8785 0726

Rodos Restaurant & Taverna (1)
10 Streatham High Road
LONDON SW16 1DB
Tel: 020 8769 2946

Sapphω Meze Bar (1)
9 Clapham High Street, Clapham North
LONDON SW4 7TS
Tel: 020 7498 9009

The Four Lanterns (1)
96 Cleveland Street, off Euston Road
LONDON W1P 5DP
Tel: 020 7387 0704

The Apollonia (1)
17a Percy Street, LONDON W1T 1DU
Tel: 020 7637 3724

Elysee Greek Restaurant (2)
13 Percy Street, off Tottenham Court Rd
LONDON W1T 9LD
Tel: 020 7636 4804

Andrea's Greek Restaurant (2)
22 Charlotte Street, nr Tottenham Court
Road, LONDON W1T 1RL
Tel: 020 7580 8971

Jimmy's Restaurant (2)
23 Frith Street, Soho,
LONDON W1V 5TS
Tel: 020 7437 9521

Kalamaras Greek Taverna (2)
66 Inverness Mews, Westminster
LONDON W2 3JQ
Tel: 020 7727 9122

Halepi Restaurant (2)
18 Leinster Terrace, LONDON W2
Tel: 020 7262 1070

Kleftiko Greek Restaurant (1)
293 Chiswick High Road,
LONDON W4 4HH
Tel: 020 8994 0305 / 8747 8391

Atlantis Restaurant (1)
86 Pitshanger Lane, Ealing
LONDON W5 1QX
Tel: 020 8810 8836

Wine & Mousaka (1)
30 Haven Green, Ealing,
LONDON W5 2NY
Tel: 020 8997 0287

Costa's Grill (2)
14 Hillgate Street, LONDON W8 7SP
Tel: 020 7229 3794

Konaki Greek Restaurant (3)
5 Coptic Street, LONDON WC1A 1NH
Tel: 020 7580 3712 / 9730

Yialousa Restaurant (2)
18 Woburn Place, LONDON WC1H 0LU
Tel: 020 7837 4748

New Rodos Restaurant (2)
59 St Giles High Street,
LONDON WC2H 8LH
Tel: 020 7836 3177

Arena Greek Restaurant (1)
307 Harrow Road, WEMBLEY
Middx HA9 6BD
Tel: 020 8902 1898

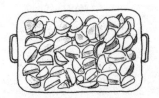

Orpheus Taverna (1)
369 Richmond Road East,
TWICKENHAM, Middx TW1 2EJ
Tel: 020 8892 3103

The Vine Taverna (1)
528-530 Victoria Road, RUISLIP
Middlesex HA4 0HB
Tel: 020 8841 5223 / 020 8845 7094

SOUTH EAST

Vineyard Steak House
64 Preston Street, BRIGHTON
East Sussex BN1 2HE
Tel: 01273 321681

Dartford Greek Taverna (2)
59-65 Hythe Street, DARTFORD
Kent DA1 1BG
Tel: 01322 271 888

Sevenoaks Greek Taverna (1)
115 London Road, SEVENOAKS
Kent TN13 1BH
Tel: 01732 465 115/ 464 624

Old Bexley Greek Taverna (5) *
82 Bexley High Street, BEXLEY
Kent DA5 1LB
Tel: 01322 554 233 / 01322 526 298

Wine & Mousaka (2)
12 Kew Green, KEW GARDENS
Surrey TW9 3BH
Tel: 020 8940 5696

Olympic Restaurant (3)
140 Frimley Road, CAMBERLEY
Surrey GU15 2QN
Tel: 01276 684 919

The Greek Vine Restaurant (3)
The Green, CLAYGATE
Surrey KT10 0JQ
Tel: 01372 465125 / 468888

Louis Restaurant (1)
17 Bridge Road EAST MOLESEY
Surrey KT8 9EU
Tel: 020 8979 2376

Salamis Taverna (1)
86 Hill Rise RICHMOND
Surrey TW10 6UB
Tel: 020 8940 7557

Sunny Restaurant Greek Taverna
58 Ham Road, WORTHING
West Sussex BN11 2QX
Tel: 01903 230061

Illustrations by Gill Tomlinson

Whilst the demographics and willingness of our subscribers to participate,
and the availability of local Greek restaurants is likely to affect the number of
recommendations received for any particular restaurant, those with 4, 5 or 6 are
highlighted as they have obviously made an impact with lovers of Greece and must
be worth a visit if you live nearby or visit the area. Our thanks for information
received, which was checked prior to publication. Sadly several recommended
Greek restaurants had closed.

History Column

Greece & Turkey - When Treaties Bring Tragedy

by Terry Cook

There are a number of historical factors which build the background to the traumatic and disastrous events in the early 1920's often known as *'The Smyrna Incident'*. To me *'incident'* is a tragic understatement of an enormous catastrophe, which created deep scars in Greek-Turkish relations, which even now, 80 years on, are very difficult for many to get over. As is often the case, the tragedy suffered by the ordinary people – Greeks, Turks, Armenians and others - was not of their making, nor did the 'people' want the changes thrust upon them by the politics of the day.

In the late years of the 19th century, the Ottoman empire was crumbling, many of its vassal states had already gained independence, and there was unrest and revolution at home and abroad. In Europe, Germany was ascending in power and beginning to scan the horizons for extensions to both lands and influence. An unhindered path to the new sources of energy in the oilfields of the middle east became a high priority and Turkey provided the perfect route. Military academies in Germany opened their doors to Turkish soldiers, eager to improve their skills in combat and conquest. With this training behind them, one group who were dissatisfied with their masters of the day, decided to act, and in 1908 the Young Turks declared a Revolutionary Government in Salonika, and proposed the adoption of the new constitution of 1876. Among them was one very able commander - Mustapha Kemal - later known as Attaturk, father of the Turks.

Meanwhile, Greece's own political turmoil, its struggles through the years of World War One and then the Balkan Wars, created a vacuum which Prime Minister Venizelos tried to turn to his own advantage. The Treaty of Sevres went a long way to fulfilling Venizelos' demands for new borders after these conflicts were ended, but it took a long time for the allies to agree. Greece should have (according to Venizelos) northern Epirus (well into Albania), Thrace going east right up to the Bosphorus Sea, Smyrna and the hinterland of Western Turkey and the Dodecanese – at that time under Italian control, and international status for the straits of Marmara and Constantinople. Because of the delay, however, and encouraged by the support of Lloyd George from Britain, Venizelos decided not to wait for the official go ahead, and in May 1919 he sent troops to occupy Smyrna, and Epirus later in the year. His argument was the need to protect the Greek nationals living in the area from reprisals from the Turks who had been severely defeated.

What both Venizelos and Lloyd George failed to notice to their ultimate cost was that Mustapha Kemal was gaining a large and strong following in Turkey for his radical view to change the fortunes of Turkey into a progressive, republican state. In August 1920 the treaty was finally signed, but it was never ratified, and the allies decided to leave Constantinople under the nominal control of the Sultan. Undeterred, Venizelos began an offensive against Kemal moving inland from Smyrna. Further upset at home, however, changed the fortunes of this endeavour - first King Alexander of Greece was fatally bitten by a monkey – he died on 25th Oct 1920. Three weeks later the Greek electorate, tired of troubles and constant warfare, decisively removed Venizelos from power in a general election, and against the advice of the allies organised a plebiscite to return King Constantine to the throne (he was the father of King Alexander, forced to abdicate in 1917).

The new Prime Minister, Gounaris, backed by the king, continued to pursue the campaign in Anatolia, but with new and inexperienced officers in charge, inadequate equipment and weapons, they did not achieve much success. Indeed, in June when they made a final assault from the River Sakaria, Kemal was able to mount a counteroffensive from a position of greater strength, and heavily defeated the Greek forces. The retreat through the summer and autumn of 1921 left the Greeks in no doubt that ultimate victory had slipped from their grasp. The winter saw them going cap in hand to the allied powers for help, but the allies had accepted that Turkey was again a force to be reckoned with. At a peace conference in Paris in March 1922, an armistice was proposed which Greece accepted. Kemal, however, said he would only accept a ceasefire if Greece agreed to evacuate all non-Muslim citizens from the Turkish mainland immediately.

This was unacceptable to the allies, so Kemal decided to force the evacuation himself - at the point of a gun. At the end of August he mounted a massive attack on Smyrna, and within ten days the city was

on fire, and those that were not slaughtered or carried off as slaves, were forced into the sea to drown. All this with a large number of allied ships anchored in the bay out of reach and under orders not to get involved. As people who could find a boat

of some sort fled for their lives, turning back all they saw was their homeland ablaze, their friends and families dying, and the west looking on and doing absolutely nothing. This was the *'incident'* that is as much a blight on the emergence of 'new' Turkey, as it is on the ineffective international diplomacy of the western powers of the day.

This Smyrna massacre was just one incident in Turkey's programme of annihilation of undesirable 'barbarian' influences, but created more public awareness of the ongoing situation. From the late 1800's there had been systematic slaughtering of first Armenians, then Pontian Greeks, then Greeks from Smyrna and Thrace, as well as other minority populations including Kurds and Syrians. Statistics quoted vary but are nothing short of genocide, and would have been much worse, were it not for the Treaty of Lausanne in 1923. The allies persuaded Turkey to agree to an exchange of 'minority' populations - nearly one and a half million Greeks were to leave Turkish soil and their homes, and some three to four hundred thousand ethnic Turks in Greece were to go to Turkey. Only a part of eastern Thrace was exempted from the enforced exchange, where the two peoples did live and still do, in harmony.

Some estimates put the number of Armenians, Greeks and others exterminated or 'disappeared without trace' through deprivation, forced labour, etc as high as three million souls over a thirty year period. What it is not possible to quantify is the longer term damage done to those uprooted, who lost their identity, their social framework in villages and families, and their self-respect as they became refugees and even outcasts in a land that may well have been their 'ethnic' home, but was to them a foreign country. Greece suffered the trauma of a sudden influx of over a million dispossessed people - the population of Athens doubled in a very short space of time. An enormous strain was put on everybody, and those who suffered most were those who had least and deserved to suffer least.

Fotis Kontoglou writing in 'Aivali - My Home Country' explained why his village did not want to flee, but had to. *"We were chased by the Turks in 1922 - there was wailing and crying all along the coastline, because people had gone down confusedly to the sea in the hope of getting away, of escaping to the nearby Greek islands. The Turks are a good and compassionate people by nature, but war is like a sickness that affects both good and bad alike, and turns them wild. On many of the beaches there were no boats, and the people just sat down together at the water's edge, and wept and shouted, for some boat to come over the open sea. But no boats came - because so many desperate people would have capsized them, and as a result the poor wretches spent all day on the rocks. To Ak Tsi they had come from the heart of Anatolia, from Adramuti, from Ivanti, from Freneli, thousands of people, women, children, old people. In Dikeli they had come down from Pergamum and the surrounding villages.*

"In my town, Aivali, there were many caiques because it was by the sea, but the people had decided not to flee, but to live with the Turks. They took the rudders off their boats so that nobody else could use them to escape. When we finally decided to leave, what to put in the boat, people or things?

"... When Sunday dawned, I got up and went to Taliani. I saw a caique coming - the captain was a Mytilene man, from Plomari, and he was looking for a charter. I told him the people of Aivali didn't want to leave, but I made an agreement with him. Next day was a fine day, and we loaded what we could in the caique, and in my small boat, which we tied behind, we loaded as much as possible and we left for the open sea. Some boats had come in from the surrounding islands, when they learned of the danger. We told them the situation and set sail for Mytilene.

"... we reached Thermi, where we off-loaded the caique. We took a house near the sea and we settled in. I gave my boat to some fisherman from Csesme – a refugee like myself, so he could go fishing to feed his children.

It was the 14th August when we fled Anatolia and became refugees. In the days that followed many more caiques came, and they disembarked many traumatised people ... Opposite we could see the mountains, and they looked as if they were weeping too ... we could see smoke ris-

ing here and there, and during the night fires burning all along the shoreline ... many times my eyes filled with tears as I sat there at the water's edge and looked over opposite, because the sea was roaring between Anatolia and the island where I was now living."

How desperate it must have been, when Greek and Turk who had lived and worked together as friends and neighbours in villages and towns throughout Anatolia, were suddenly cast as enemies by outsiders. Maria Katsidou-Symeonidou was just four years old when one day in 1918 in her village of Mourasoul she recalls: *"I remember the deportations well - I saw my father in the village square. I ran to him and asked for the pie he brought me every day from the family-owned mill. He replied 'O my child, the Turks are going to kill me and you will not see me again.' He told me to get mother to prepare some food and clothes for him to take - that was the last we saw of him. He was killed along with ten other men from the village. I remember the time a Turk came and warned our village: 'All the young men should leave, because Topal Osman is coming'. Those that left were saved, but they still killed fifteen men including the teacher, the village president and the priest. With over three hundred others from surrounding villages, they were bound, murdered and cast into the river. I still remember the echoes of the shots - it took nine days to recover all the bodies and bury them.*

"Around Easter 1920, the Turkish army came and told us to take everything we could carry. On the deportation march, the Turkish guards would rape the women ... we were taken to a place without water ... many died of thirst. The killings only stopped in 1923 with the exchange of populations - I came to Hellas, an orphan."

Sophia Stambolidou was born in Tsegeri in 1910 and says of her ordeal: *"I remember when the Turkish army had encircled us ... our fighters said the women and children must be moved to a safer place. Before we left, however, they agreed to smother the very young, as they feared the cries of babies would betray us and none would survive – one was my nephew. One father could not bring himself to smother his little girl, so he left her*

behind. A few days later we found her alive, and she eventually came to Hellas with us. The group moved on, but when the Turks found the smothered infants, they froze with fear, realising just how determined were our fighters, prepared to do whatever it took. We came to Hellas in 1923 with the exchange of populations via Roumania and Thessalonika."

Farewell Anatolia a novel by Dido Sotiriou is just one of many books which recounts in heart-rending ways just what the people of those times went through, as they were forced to leave their homes, their families and their friends - both Greek and Turkish. The pain and torture, the wanton destruction and above all the total pointlessness of it all - and what was gained?

Many words have been written about the personal suffering of ordinary people at this time, and although I have included some here to try to explain the horrors that were taking place, no amount of talk can ever repair the damage that was done to humanity at that time. We can only mourn, and move on vowing never to let this kind of thing happen again. We must not be discouraged that it did happen again and again throughout the twentieth century, and is still happening today.

It is our duty as members of the human race to stamp out the kind of bitterness, racial violence and antagonism that seems so often to beset us. Let us make a treaty with ourselves and our fellow man, whoever he might be, that we will live together in peace without the need for the bullet and murder to solve our differences. This is the kind of treaty that does NOT bring tragedy to mankind.

(Archive pictures from website with permission)

The Acropolis of Athens *by Mary Lambell*

Retired classics teacher, Mary Lambell, is well qualified for this contribution on ancient Greek sites. Here she tells us about the main buildings of the Athens Acropolis and the background to statues and friezes on the site or in museums.

Clipart from IMSI

Probably the most visited ancient site in the whole of Greece, the Acropolis, is very different now from its 5th century BC appearance, not only because the temples are in ruins. Like all other religious sanctuaries the site was crammed with buildings and statues in the Golden Age of Ancient Greece.

A c r o p o l i s (Ακρόπολη) means citadel (άκρο-top, πόλη-city, town), so its origin was defensive, being the stronghold, the 'high city', where the early kings lived. Probably only in the 6th century BC did it become a religious place. The earliest temple remains belong to about 525BC. This and another unfinished temple built to celebrate the Greek victory at Marathon in 490BC, were destroyed by the Persians when they invaded Athens shortly before the battle of Salamis in 480BC. Initially the Athenians decided not to rebuild, but to leave the ruins as a reminder of what had happened, but Pericles, the leading politician of the day, suggested that the Acropolis should be redeveloped as a monument to Athens' achievements. A similar situation today perhaps is the debate about what to do with the site of the World Trade Center. Pericles devised a grand new scheme, financed to a large extent by contributions from Athens' allies.

Included in the plan were the Propylaia, (the grand entrance), and the three temples visible today, as well as many other structures now gone.

Acropolis of Athens Today

The Propylaia, built between 437 and 432BC was designed by Mnesikles. Its axis was aligned to the Parthenon (already built) and it faced towards the island of Salamis, scene of the Greek victory over the Persians in 480BC. It was intended to be imposing, and had to be large enough to accommodate the passage of 100 oxen which were led up to be sacrificed at the Panathenaic Festival. From the front and rear its appearance was of a Doric temple, but it should have been flanked by wings on each side. The north wing was called the *pinakotheke*, (picture gallery) as it housed paintings by the famous painter Polygnotus. It was also used probably as a dining room for ritual meals at festivals. The south wing was never completed. Inside is a passageway with three Ionic columns each side.

Just outside this entrance, steps led up to the right to an artificial bastion on which was built the little **Temple of Athena Nike**, an excellent example of Ionic architecture, designed by Kallikrates. Nike means victory, and the temple was built between 427 and 424BC, as a thank-offering to the goddess for victory over the Persians, and in the hope that she would give them victory over the Spartans, whom they were currently fighting in the Peloponnesian War (431-404BC). Unfortunately she did not! The sculpture round the frieze depicted a battle, probably the Persian War. Some of this is now in the British Museum.

The most obvious building on the Acropolis when seen from afar and the first thing you see as you enter through the Propylaia is the **Parthenon.** It

was the first temple to be built in Pericles' scheme, between 447 and 438BC. Its full title is the Temple of Athena Parthenos, Athena the Virgin. It was designed by Iktinos and Kallikrates, with Pheidias responsible for the sculptural elements. Inside was a chryselephantine (gold and ivory) statue of the goddess, made by Pheidias and much admired in ancient times. Nothing remains of this now, only copies which do not give more than an idea what it would have looked like.

Basically a Doric temple, with traditional sculpted metopes and triglyphs forming the exterior frieze, it had an additional continuous frieze round the outside of the naos (the inner room). All the sculptural decoration had a significance either political or religious. The east pediment, (gable end), over the main entrance, contained a representation of the birth of Athena, from Zeus' head, with the other gods looking on in amazement. According to the legend, Zeus swallowed Metis, his wife, when she was pregnant; he subsequently had a headache, and Hephaistos, the god of metalworkers, split his head with an axe, and out came Athena, fully grown and fully armed! No wonder Zeus had a headache!

The west pediment told the story of Athena's contest with Poseidon for supremacy over Athens. Poseidon struck the rock of the Acropolis with his trident, and a spring of water appeared, unfortunately salt water! Athena planted her spear in the ground and an olive tree sprouted. The other gods judged her the winner. It was the olive which was largely responsible for Athens' great wealth. Poseidon did not lose out altogether though: as to him was attributed Athens' supremacy at sea, essential for trade and warfare. The pedimental sculptures had been severely damaged before Lord

Elgin took them to Britain. Drawings made earlier are the main source of our knowledge of them.

The metopes all depict battles, different on each side: Lapiths and Centaurs, gods and giants, Greeks and Amazons, Greeks and Trojans. Some of the Lapiths and Centaurs are in the British Museum. The legend is that the Centaurs, half man, half horse, were invited to the wedding of Pirithous, king of their neighbours the Lapiths. They behaved well until, under the influence of drink, they tried to abduct the bride and the other women. The ensuing battle ended in victory for the Lapiths. All these battles were symbolic of the triumph of civilisation over barbarism, ie Greeks over Persians! It is the sculptures from the Parthenon which the Greeks want returned from the British Museum to their original home, quite rightly I feel.

The continuous frieze, probably the best known of the sculptures, depicts the Panathenaic procession, which took place every four years at the Great Panathenaia, the festival in honour of Athena. This festival was the most important in the Athenian calendar, as it celebrated their patron goddess, and had political overtones, in that they could show off their city to their allies. It featured competitions of music, recitations of Homer and athletics, culminating in a great procession; this began at one of the main city gates, crossed the Agora and finally reached the Acropolis, where the 100 oxen were sacrificed and a new robe (peplos) was presented to the goddess to be put on the statue of her in the Erechtheion. The frieze shows horsemen, chariots, young men and girls, priests and cattle, finishing above the east, main entrance where the gods are depicted, on a larger scale, watching the proceedings. In the British Museum a misleading impression is given as the frieze should run round the outside, not inside. The quality of carving is superb: the sculptor has created an impression of great depth in only 2.5 inches of marble.

The third temple, **the Erechtheion**, is the most complex in design, and the last built of the three (421-406BC). Because it had to accommodate several different ancient shrines, and be on two levels, the design is irregular, with three porches rather than the normal two. It was dedicated to Erechtheus, an early king of Athens, as well as to Athena Polias (protector of the city), and Poseidon. Its north porch was supposed to contain the marks of Poseidon's trident (see legend above) and had an opening in its roof in case he should strike again! Inside was the pool he created and just outside the west wall was Athena's olive tree. There is an olive tree there to this day.

Caryatid Porch

An unusual feature is the south porch, with girls (known as Caryatids), instead of columns supporting the roof. It was the statue of Athena in this temple, (very old and venerable, supposedly fallen from heaven!) which was given the new robe at the festival. The temple is Ionic and very elegant in its design, rich with carved decoration.

Between the Parthenon and the Erechtheion was a huge altar, where the oxen were sacrificed. Between the Propylaia and the Erechtheion was a great bronze statue, by Pheidias, 40 feet high, of Athena Promachos, Athena who fought for Athens. This statue too looked out towards Salamis, only the base now remains. The Acropolis would have been full of colour: sculpture and architectural details were painted in bright colours. This may not be to our taste, but think of the brightly painted churches in Greece today which we so much admire and photograph.

The Acropolis was not only a religious sanctuary, dedicated mainly to Athena the goddess of Athens, celebrating her life and festival, but also it made a political statement. The Parthenon was a national monument - then as well as now - celebrating victory over Persia and proclaiming the city's greatness. This perhaps explains why it is so important to the Greeks to have their sculptures returned to them.

It is ironic that by the end of the 5th century BC Athens had been defeated by Sparta. Her 'golden age' was over.

Pioneering Women in Salonika World War I

by Carol Coles

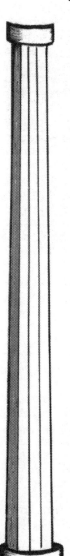

Carol works as an Information Analyst in the NHS in Chester. She was researching the history of a local Victorian Asylum for a personal local history project and came across a reference to a female doctor who went to Serbia in World War I, and so she was sidetracked into finding out about what happened in Salonika at that time.

Mention World War 1 to people and it conjures up images of miles of trenches and stalemate battles fought in the mud, not cosmopolitan Thessaloniki (at that time known as Salonika) and the plains of Macedonia. However it was here that a group of remarkable women endeavoured to do their part during the War in Europe.

World War 1 broke out in August 1914 when the assassination of the Austrian Archduke Ferdinand by a Bosnian student resulted in the outbreak of a conflict that involved all the major European powers. Greece was officially neutral but its Prime Minister, Venizelos, was strongly pro-Ally.

As early as Spring 1915 representatives of the Allies operated in Serbia and the surrounding areas in humanitarian work principally in the operation of field hospitals. One of the key organisations involved in this work was the Scottish Women's Hospitals (SWH) founded in Edinburgh by Elsie Ingles. During 1915 conditions in Serbia deteriorated and by November as the Austrians and Bulgarians advanced the Serbian Army was in retreat. Members of the SWH were caught up in the retreat while others stayed in Serbia under the occupying powers until early 1916 when they were repatriated to Britain. The retreat during November and December over the Prokletiji Mountains between Kosovo and Albania became the stuff of legend due to the appalling conditions endured by military and civilians alike.

After the fall of Serbia the Allies' only foothold in the Balkans was the port of Salonika. Too late to assist the Serbian effort the Allies sent a military force which became known disparagingly as 'The Gardeners of Salonika' because there was so little for them to do against the enemy which held the mountains including Mount Kaimaktsalan (Mount Kajmakchalan) which surround Macedonia. In the diaries of women who came to work in the Allied hospitals in Salonika there are references to the sound of gunfire in the mountains being heard even in the city.

In the autumn of 1915 the SWH sent a unit to Salonika to establish a hospital under the control of Dr Louise McIlory. This was the 'Girton and Newnham Unit' so named because the money to finance it was raised by the two Cambridge women's colleges. The Unit was given a temporary site close to the sea in which to establish its hospital. It was to stay in this low lying site, prone to flooding, until the Spring of 1918 when it moved to a larger site enabling expansion of the facilities to 500 beds and the establishment of an orthopaedic unit. The SWH were not the only organisation to establish a hospital in Salonika. There were others run by the Allied military and staffed by orders such as the Queen Alexandra's Imperial Military Nursing Service (QAIMNS). The majority of these hospitals were temporary structures of wood huts and tents. The SWH established a further hospital at Ostrovo (now Arnissa) close to Limni Vegoritidha in northern Macedonia. This was referred to as the 'American Unit' as that was where the money to finance it had been raised. Late in 1916 a dressing station was established at Dobroveni (in what is now the Former Yugoslav Republic of Macedonia) just behind the front line so that wounded soldiers could get some kind of medical help more quickly. With the difficult mountainous terrain it could take 48 hours to get a wounded soldier to the Salonika hospital.

The SWH was founded in Edinburgh in 1914 but its members were not exclusively Scottish nor was there a ban on men working in supportive roles. However the doctors, nurses, orderlies and ambulance drivers were all women. They came from across Britain and from parts of the Empire principally Australia and New Zealand. Dr Agnes Bennett who commanded the SWH hospital in Ostrovo came from Australia but had met Elsie Ingles when she was studying in Edinburgh. These woman doctors operated in the tented hospitals close to the front line. Dr Anna Muncaster, who had been on the retreat from Serbia, worked at Ostrovo and Dobroveni. The Royal Medico-Psychological Association, in an appreciation written after her death in 1930, made reference to her calmness and courage operating under fire at Dobroveni. Female ambulance drivers negotiated the treacherous mountain roads, nurses and orderlies dealt with the wounded men of the multi national Allied forces. Even in Salonika it was not completely safe and there was a constant threat of German bombing raids. Edith Moor a QAIMNS nurse at the 43rd General Hospital wrote in her diary about a raid where some of the bombs aimed at the ordnance hit the 29th General Hospital killing 9 patients and injuring about 17 more.

However all was not gloom, Salonika was a bustling vibrant front line city full of representatives of a multitude of nationalities. The officers of the Allied forces congregated at Floca's café night and day. One of the SWH's doctors thought that the only nationalities she had not seen were Eskimos, Pigmies or Aborigines!

At Salonika and Ostrovo the women of the SWH had parties complete with Scottish dancing especially at Christmas and New Year. When it was warmer there were opportunities to swim in the lake or go horse riding in the countryside surrounding Ostrovo. In summer the weather was hot and stifling. The lack of rain in August 1917 meant that when fire broke out in the old Turkish quarter of Salonika it spread rapidly resulting in the destruction of 95,000 homes. Sparks fell on the tents of the SWH hospital but fortunately the wind changed direction so there was no serious damage.

By the summer of 1918 the tide was turning in the War with the Allied offensive in Macedonia starting on the 15th September and by early October the conflict in the Balkans was over. In Salonika the SWH hospital stayed until after the end of the War but the American Unit moved from Ostrovo to Vranja in Serbia during the autumn of 1918.

After the War many members of the SWH, like Dr Louise McIlroy, went on to have distinguished careers. In 1920 she was appointed Consultant in obstetrics and gynaecology at the Royal Free Hospital in London and Professor at the London School of Medicine for Women. In 1929 she was made a Dame for her services to medicine. Dr Agnes Bennett returned to her post as chief medical officer at St Helens maternity hospital in Wellington. She had a successful career in Australia and Britain, being awarded a DBE in 1948.

However the majority of the women who had worked in Salonika and Ostrovo returned to obscurity and the restrictions of women's lives in the post War period. After nursing under fire, driving ambulances and encountering the cosmopolitan world of Northern Greece it is hard to imagine how they settled back into family life in Britain. It is only in recent years with the increased interest in women's history that their remarkable work is being rediscovered.

Various sources principally Leah Leneman "In the Service of Life" Mercat Press 1994 ISBN 1873644264 £9.99 (still available)

Living the Life of the Gods *by Sylvia Cook*

Life on Mount Olympos must have been one long party for Zeus and his relations. When they weren't sampling the wines of junior god Dionysos or eating ambrosia, they were thinking up trials for their protégé heroes on earth, plotting to upset the schemes of the other gods, sending 'signs' to show people what they must do when they felt like it, or planning to drop down on the mere mortals in some form or other to take advantage for a bit of fun or for personal gain.

The Greek gods were never seen as perfect - which gave them a lot of leeway! They were all-powerful and immortal. Mortals had to look up to them and to obey their commands, or do what they thought would please the gods to make their own lives better. The priests and priestesses of the temples to individual gods would suggest how their god should be pleased or appeased and interpret the perceived signs from the gods. Animals were often sacrificed to the gods and gifts given to them, so the priests did alright from perpetuating an image of gods who needed to be pampered.

Clipart from IMSI

The gods commanded the forces of nature - wind, rain, sun, cloud and earthquakes. They could ensure a good harvest or they could upset the weather at critical times and destroy the crops if they were made angry.

The gods could control peoples' emotions - making a beautiful maiden fall in love with a lucky man, or a promising young man to pursue his own downfall. They could help an athlete to win a race or cause a limb to break so that a combatant was defeated. The gods also controlled animals and would often appear on earth in the form of a bird or animal - so people imagined they saw or heard the gods quite regularly. The gods could be blamed for anything that went wrong, or anything that went right.

The gods were believed to live in the sky or on Mount Olympos in Thessaly - which reached pretty far into the sky from where mere mortals lived. Although powerful, they were seen as human with human failings and feelings. Each god or goddess had an individual character and a role to play.

Zeus, the most powerful god, ruler of the other gods, was also responsible for thunder and lightning (often portrayed carrying a thunderbolt, ready to throw, wherever he went) and the heavens. Although married to his sister Hera (the gods were all one family, so incest was not considered abnormal), he had an eye for the ladies and liked to have his wicked way with pretty mortals and goddesses. He did not worry about deceiving his wife, who could be very jealous - as Zeus he could contrive ways to hide his mistresses from her, as he did with a bit of help from brother Poseidon when Leto gave birth to his son Apollo on the newly formed island of Delos which 'appeared in the waves' to shelter her.

Poseidon wielded much power over mortals being god of the sea and storms, as well as having power to shake the earth and to control horses. He was less successful in competition against his fellow gods - losing out to Athena when his gift of a spring on the Acropolis of Athens was deemed less worthy than her gift of an olive tree. He tried the opposite by causing drought in Argolis, but lost out here to Hera. He had a quarrelsome nature and was easily angered, so seafarers always needed to appease him.

Hera, as wife of the 'chief'' god, was queen of the gods and responsible for looking after the fate of women and childbirth - but woe betide any woman who had a dalliance with her husband! She constantly spied on Zeus and persecuted his mistresses and their offspring. One wonders when she had time to answer the prayers and look after other mortal women. Perhaps why women had few rights and no education in ancient Greece.

Sister **Hestia** was probably more useful to women than Hera. As goddess of the hearth she looked after people in their homes and generally tried to keep out of the quarrels of the other gods and to keep the peace. She was a virgin and a bit of a goody-goody, so there are few stories about her.

Hades, brother of Zeus and god of the underworld, did not enjoy the fun and games on Mount Olympos with the other gods, although he was said to venture from his underground home occasionally when overcome by lust. Once the dead entered his domain they did not escape.

Demeter also a sister to Zeus was the devoted hard working goddess of plants and the harvest. She was also responsible for teaching newlyweds although she had no husband of her own. She had two children to Zeus and another to the Titan Iacchus - killed in his jealousy by Zeus. Her daughter from Zeus was abducted by Hades. Demeter grieved, chilling the earth and killing all crops, so an agreement was reached that Persephone spend just part of each year in the underworld, during which time Demeter stopped work and winter fell until her daughter was returned each Spring.

Aphrodite, the daughter of Uranus, was goddess of love and beauty. She was emotional and a romantic trying to ensure the course of true love ran smoothly, or creating loving emotions and liaisons between the unsuspecting. Her magic girdle made everyone fall in love with the wearer - usually herself. She spurned the advances of Zeus, was married off to the ugly Hephaestus but went on to have many romantic entanglements amongst the other gods and a few special mortals including Adonis.

Apollo was probably the most powerful of the children of Zeus. God of the sun, light, prophecy, music, poetry, art and even medicine - he had a lot to do. He was fed on nectar and ambrosia as a baby and took to using a bow and arrows from an early age with great effect, but also won musical contests and seduced nymphs and women and even Hyacinthus - a boy.

Artemis was goddess of hunting, the moon and protector of children. She hung around with her brother Apollo and helped him out of scrapes from time to time. She was fearless and chaste - but still chased.

Goddess of wisdom and war, **Athena** was a great inventor and also taught mathematics. Born from Zeus' head in some stories, she must have been given an extra share of brains. Unlike Ares, her interest in war was to avoid bloodshed and to settle disputes peacefully. Athena was modest, yet generous offering comfort and guidance to all.

At first known as god of storms and tempests, **Ares** son of Zeus and Hera, became god of war. He was single minded and cared only for war enjoying the slaughter and terror of battle. He was terrifying, but also made mistakes and was often wounded. One of Aphrodite's lovers, he fathered several of her children - so presumably was not warmongering all the time.

Hephaestus was the unfortunate ugly god of fire and metal workers. One wonders if he got to join in many parties with the other immortals. His mother Hera was disgusted by the sight of him and threw him into the sea when he was born and later Zeus broke his leg making him permanently lame when he kicked him out of Olympos and on to the island of Lemnos. Hopefully as a blacksmith he was able to be a useful god for those of that profession.

Hermes the messenger god, son of Zeus and Maia, supposedly grew very quickly and even slipped out the day he was born, stealing a herd of cows from Apollo in his search for adventure. He slaughtered two, dividing these into 12 portions to sacrifice to the gods (who were only 11 until then) eating the twelfth portion himself. He made up with Apollo by giving him his newly invented lyre and a pipe to play sweet music. His father Zeus liked this son and gave him winged sandals to carry him swiftly to protect travellers.

The Olympian gods (excluding Hades who mostly stayed below ground) had many lesser gods to dine and have fun with, each with a different nature and their own duties to perform. Life was never dull on Mount Olympos.

Clipart from IMSI

The Truth Behind the Myth of Jason *by Terry Cook*

The Greek tradition of 'myth' to recount history and explain the mysteries of life, is well-known to anyone who has an interest in Greece. Sometimes, however, the fantasy side or 'false' myth detracts from the underlying truth or history being conveyed, because it is too difficult to perceive in the 'story'. Even the great philosophers and historians of early Greece did not profess to understand all myth - and that which was beyond them, they just accepted as true, or at least that it contained truth which they could not see right away. So without getting bogged down in too many details of Jason's story, let's look for the point or lesson the story reveals.

A baby doomed to die by his power-hungry uncle, is brought up in secret by a half man /half animal benefactor (Chiron the Centaur who taught many of the ancient heroes). He returns to claim his birthright as king of Iolcus in Central Greece. To prove his worth (or just to get rid of him) he is set an impossible task - to reclaim the Golden Fleece from the far side of the known world.

To achieve success, which he is completely confident of doing, he has *the best and fastest ship built that is known to man* at that time, and he selects the strongest and bravest men to crew her and to be his companions on this great voyage of adventure and discovery. Overcoming all manner of obstacles along the way, he reaches the place of final challenge, only to be met with yet more impossible tasks to perform in order to achieve his goal.

Undeterred, he presses on and for his determination to see 'right' prevail, he is afforded the help of the gods, of Hera in particular. She, being the 'mother' of the gods, was upset to the point of distraction that the aforementioned uncle of Jason - now King Pelias - had refused to offer the sacrifices to her she felt were her due. Nothing is ever straight forward in these matters, however, so she engages the skills of Aphrodite, who in turn subcontracts the task to Eros, to manipulate the life of Jason (not to mention those with him) to get her own revenge.

Now the twist - Medea is the sorceress daughter of King Aietes of Colchis (that's on the eastern shores of the Black Sea), and by all accounts is not a very nice person to know. Enter Eros with his world-famous little arrows, and swift as you can say 'Piccadilly Circus' Medea's hard heart has turned to jelly for the love of our hero Jason. Timing is always said to be of the essence, and when the gods are involved, they should know when and where is the best move. It was Medea's father who had the privilege of keeping the 'golden fleece' and in order to win her prince, she did everything she could to influence the successful outcome of Jason's quest.

From quiet words in her father's ear to se-cret potions and 'insider information' as to the whereabouts of the fleece and sub-duing the dragon, Medea was certainly a useful ally to have. The minor matter of murdering her own brother and throwing his dismembered body into the sea to dis-tract her father from pursuing them, was a small price to pay, in her mind, to win her man. When at last, after even more extravagant adventures, they finally returned to Iolcus, Medea's help was again enlisted to remove Pelias from the throne. This time her twisted mind used the king's daughters to commit the murder of their own father by devi-ous trickery.

But alas, her days seemed by now to be numbered since Jason (maybe at last repudiating Medea for her excesses of wickedness) had fallen in love with a local lass, whom he determined to marry. *'Hell hath no fury like a woman scorned'*, they say, and Medea was certainly no exception. She sent a 'gift' to the bride-to-be, a beautiful wedding dress, no doubt pretend-ing it to be a peace-offering with no hard feelings. The dress, though, was laced with poison which burst into flames when she put it on, thus doubly ensuring the removal of her adversary in love.

Distraught by the knowledge that this had not in fact regained the love of Jason but only forced him away for good, Medea then killed her own two children - Jason's sons - and fled in her chariot drawn by dragons. Jason, beside himself with grief and distress, went from one despair to another, until a lonely, friendless old man, he returned to where his great ship of discovery lay rotting, maybe to remember past achievements and glory. As he sat beneath her prow, was it Medea, or maybe a god, touched the dilapi-dated structure and caused the once magnificent edifice of Athena - said to have the magical property of prophesying with human voice - to fall on him so ending the history of the triumphs and tragedies of one of ancient Greece's greatest heroes.

So the lesson would seem to be, however good the cause, we may be sure that if we let external forces control the way we act, we may make history - but if we adopt unfair means to justify the end we will have to pay the price. Society and life around will move on, maybe with a little help from those prepared to succeed, maybe with the occasional treasure of a 'golden fleece', but don't bank on everything turning out the way you planned - the gods may have their own agenda, and you - however much a hero of the day - are just a pawn in their great scheme. Or maybe not!

...the best and fastest ship known to man...

Jason's ship - The Argo, named after its builder - was the height of technological maritime development of the day. Whether in fact an actual ship, or a description of how far shipbuilding had advanced at the time, is not relevant to the story.

The ship was long and slim for speed - powered by 50 to 60 oarsmen, who sat low in the hull. There was no deck nor excess superstructure, so it could be easily carried over land when necessary.

Built from oak and pine from the Pelion Mountains, it was strong and reliable - but the added feature from the goddess Athena of a beam from the oak of Dodona for the prow, capable of speaking oracles in human voice, is what really gave it the edge. Reality, or to show how good the onboard navigation system was, since lined up with the steering oar or rudder at the bow, it created a compass which, with the stars, guided the sailors very precisely.

from BullFinch's Mythology

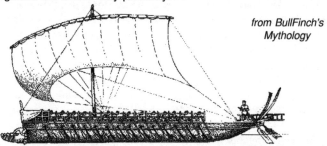

It was possibly the advanced design of the Argo, which made it the first ship capable of passing unscathed through the 'clashing rocks' - the Symplegades, a narrow strait at the entrance to the Bosphorus Sea. Legend had it that whenever the older, more round and unmanageable vessels attempted to pass, the rocks would crash together, smashing them into pieces.

It was Phineus, in thanks for ridding him of the Harpies, who advised Jason to send a dove through the misty channel first, and then quickly slip through behind before the rocks could reclose. In all probability, the 'dove' was a small pilot boat sent to find the safest passage, much as pilots do in busy or difficult harbours today. So the 'myth' of the Argonauts was simply demonstrating the great seamanship and maritime prowess which the ancient Greeks had attained.

Adventures on Jason's Journey *by Terry & Sylvia Cook*

So Jason set off on his quest, to bring back the Golden Fleece to Iolcus to prove himself to Pelias - his uncle. Having made their way round the northern coastline of Greece, to relieve the boredom of the crew, Heracles, one of the Argonaut companions, suggested they have a contest to see who could row the fastest. These lusty crewmen eagerly took up the challenge and the Argo sped onwards, until one by one they tired and dropped out. At last only Jason and Heracles were left, and soon Jason too succumbed to Heracles' superior strength. Left powering the ship with only one oar, it too finally gave way and snapped in half.

Some say it was Limnos, or maybe Chios, or even the mainland of Asia Minor, where they hauled their ship ashore, weary and in need of fresh water. Heracles sent his squire Hylas in search of supplies, but when he did not return, set off to find him. Beguiled by a nymph, Hylas was dragged down into the spring where she lived - or maybe, overanxious to drink the clear water, he slipped and drowned in the deep pool. But as Heracles wandered the island seeking his companion, Jason and the other crew members were entertained for twelve days by the local population, all women. They had lost their men some years earlier because Aphrodite had temporarily afflicted them with bad breath for not doing her due reverence, so the men went fishing and found Thracian girls!

Whatever it was that had decimated the male population, the inclement weather which kept the men there must have seemed a gift from the gods! Heracles it seems, found entertainment of his own, although one story says he had to continue with his 'labours', and when he did not return to the Argo, Jason at last made the decision to continue without him.

There were problems all along the way which Jason or one of his skilled Argonauts would resolve. Just a short while after they attended the marriage feast of King Kyzikos, they came ashore on the other side of his island to shelter, but were attacked unexpectedly, sadly killing their friend King Kyzikos, who thought they were pirates.

Later an aggressive and haughty King Amykos, of Bebrykos challenged them to a boxing match. Polydeukes, twin brother of Kastor and Olympic boxing champion, volunteered and after a ferocious fight, killed the king.

Then at Salmydessus, in Eastern Thrace, King Phineus was wasting away through lack of nourishment. As a punishment for some misdemeanour he was not only blinded but plagued by wild flying creatures with gruesome faces, who ate most of his food and left the rest inedible. Fortunately, two of the argonauts were descendants of Borea - the north wind - and could fly. They chased the unwanted guests, the Harpies, away for good and Phineus was freed from his torture.

They got through the clashing rocks and sailed eastwards. The other side they rescued four ship-wrecked mariners who were clinging to wreckage and their lives. They were grandsons of Aietes, King of Colchis - which was of course where Jason was heading. They did afford Jason access to the king, but he was not prepared to hand over the Golden Fleece in return for the services of the Argonauts. Only on youngest daughter Medea's suggestion did he set an 'impossible task' - to yoke his two fire breathing bulls and to plough a

From Nicolas-Andre Monsiau Painting (1754-1837) Jason Yokes the Bulls

field with them, planting a bag of dragon's teeth. Medea, in love with Jason, gave him a special lotion to protect him from the fire breath so he accomplished the task, but from each dragon's tooth an armed warrior sprang up. Jason flung stones at them from behind a rock and they ended up fighting amongst themselves until all were dead.

Still King Aietes did not want to relinquish the fleece, but Medea took Jason to the fleece at night. It was guarded by a fierce dragon who Medea charmed to sleep enabling Jason to take the fleece. They escaped, again with the help of Medea who accompanied them to claim her prize - Jason.

The fleece itself is quite easily explained - in mythology it was the fleece of a golden ram from the gods, but in reality particles of gold could be found in streams flowing from the mountains and a good way of collecting them was to tie a fleece across the stream, trapping the gold. This ram's fleece must have been a particularly successful trap and had probably been offered to the gods.

The journey back from acquiring the Golden Fleece was an epic one; some accounts relate that the intrepid explorers went via the major river networks of Europe, getting as far north as Scandinavia, and returning past Britain, Spain and detouring through north Africa before arriving back in Greece.

Most stories of Jason skip the details of the return journey, and cut straight to the finale which could have omitted a period of many years. Suffice to say that the Jason myths most certainly contain much of the historical background of ancient Greece, even if their over-dramatising in parts brings a high degree of scepticism as to which bits are myth and which were reality.

Greek Language

Evolution of the Greek Language *by Sylvia Cook*

Greek is one of the oldest languages in the world today, but the Ancient Greek of Homer (7th century BC), whose poetic verse form would not have been the common speech of the day, has evolved through many variations to the still changing Greek of today.

Greek began as a spoken language, with a syllabic script in Mycenaean times, but an alphabet much like today's began to evolve in classical times (8th to 4th centuries BC). There were different dialects then, but merchants could communicate. The *Ionic* dialect was more prevalent at first, evolving into greater use of the *Attic* dialect. This was the form of language spread by Alexander the Great as he extended the Greek empire.

Greek continued to evolve and change, incorporating words from Latin and Semitic languages, forming a new dialect 'Hellenistic *Kini (Κοινή)*' - the 'common' dialect. The New Testament was written in *Kini*, but some scholars continued to prefer the *Attic* dialect for their writings. Modern *Demotic* (popular) Greek is a descendent of this dialect and continued to borrow everyday words from other languages. The more archaic written form of the Greek language evolved in parallel and became known as *Katharevusa* (from καθαρός, meaning purity). It was based on Classical Greek and had none of the words loaned from Latin, Turkish and other sources. It was purist and incomprehensible to most Greeks, but in 1821 was adopted as the official Greek language of government and scholars in the new independent Greece.

However, Athenian Greek or *Demotic* grew as the spoken language and around 1900 became the established literary language as renowned writers wanted to reach more people. It also became established in schools, but *Katharevusa* continued as the official language for government documents, academic papers and was often still seen on shop signs and elsewhere.

In 1976 *Demotic* became the official language in schools and in 1977 was proclaimed as the only official language of Greece. Finally in 1982 just one accented syllable for words was introduced and some aspects of grammar simplified. Old Greek (even *Demotic*) had several different accents and 'breathings' which you may see in older books. Today some *Katharevusa* words are still used, either because they were common to both languages, or for effect - rather as we still use some archaic forms such as *'Olde Worlde'* in English! Άσπρο is demotic for white, Κρασί is wine, and although you ask for 'άσπρο κρασί', the bottle will say 'λευκός οίνος' which are *Katharevusa* words. You will also see the legacy of *Katharevusa* in village names.

Greek may not seem as easy as 'abc' coming from a Latin alphabet language, but it is easier now to learn and speak Greek than ever before.

What's in a Name? *Sylvia Cook*

Did you know?

patriarch

the father or head of a tribe
is a Greek word from

πατριά = clan *and*
αρχή = ruler

Do you get confused when it seems that people have more than one name? Sometimes the local barman is Kostas, and sometimes Kosta, Yannis becomes Yianni, Petros, Petro, etc. Unlike English where a name is a name and that's it, in Greek a name is treated the same way as any other noun. So if **Kostas** is the subject of a sentence (ie you are talking about him to someone) then there is an 's' at the end, but if you are talking *to* him it is **Kosta**. Many Greek male names end in 's' so they are easy to learn.

As the subject his name should be preceded by 'the' - '**ο Κώστας**'. Most other name endings, particularly female names, are the same for all forms of speech, but all should have ο (masculine) or η *'i'* (feminine) in front when the name is the subject of the sentence.

But ... just to confuse you when you thought you had got this simple point ... surnames can change. Many Greek women today retain their maiden surnames but if referred to as Mrs followed by their husband's surname, the ending will change for the woman. So it's **Kyrios (Mr) Papadopoulos** and **Kyria (Mrs) Papadopoulou** (the wife *of* Mr Papadopoulos) - Κύριος Παπαδόπουλος και Κύρια Παπαδοπούλου.

Note that when you are talking *about* Mr Papadopoulos he is **o Kyrios**, but if you are talking *to* him the above described rule applies and he becomes **Kyrie Papadopoule** *(Κύριε Παπαδόπουλε)*. As with names ending in 'α', his wife's title does not change if talking *to* her.

Common Greek Place Names *by Sylvia Cook*

When you go to a new Greek island or mainland area, it often seems as if they all have the same place names. Maybe this is not so surprising as towns or villages are often named after the saint's name of the local church, or some distinguishing natural feature, or the work that was carried out in the area. When you know what the name means it can help to remember it or know what kind of terrain to expect.

Here are the origins or meanings of town or village names you may come across - some from modern Greek, some from earlier forms of the Greek language. The endings can vary.

Achladeri /Αχλαδερή - αχλαδιά = pear tree

Aghia / Αγία followed by female saint's name - Αγία = saint (feminine form)

Aghios / Άγιος followed by male saint's name - Άγιος = saint (male form)

Akrotiri / Ακρωτήρι = cape

Aliki / Αλυκή = salt flats or salt works

Anemotia /Ανεμότια, Anemoutsa / Ανεμούτσα - άνεμος = wind

Aspro .../ Άσπρο ... = white (often prefix eg white tower, white island)

Chrissi Akti / Χρυσή Ακτή = golden beach

Fanari/Φανάρι = lamp or light

Faros /Φάρος = lighthouse

Filia / Φιλία = friendship

Gialos / Γιαλός = seashore, beach

Hora / Χώρα = country, land, but also often used for the inland main town

Horio / Χωριό = village (usually main village on small island)

Kambos / Κάμπος = plain (often flat farming area)

Kastro / Κάστρο = castle

Keramio / Κεράμιο, Keramia/ Κεραμεία - κεραμική = pottery, ceramic

Lefka / Λεύκα = poplar tree,

Lefkos / Λευκός = white or blank (from Katharevusa) - often a prefix

Limni / Λίμνη = lake or pool

> **See offers page for Ectaco English-Greek talking translators at discounted prices for Greek-o-File readers.**

Limani / Λιμάνι = harbour, port, or just seafront

Loutra / Λουτρά, Loutraki / Λουτράκι - λουτρόν = bathing

Neohori / Νεοχώρι = new village (Neo meaning 'new' is often a prefix)

Ormos / Όρμος, Ormoú = bay, or bay of

Paleohori /Παλαιοχώρι = old village, (Paleo meaning 'old' is a common prefix for many village names)

Paralia /Παραλία = coast

Petra / Πέτρα = stone or rock

Pigi / Πηγή = spring Pigadi/ Πηγάδι = well

Pirgos / Πύργος = castle, tower

Potami / Ποτάμι, Potamos / Ποταμός = river

Skala / Σκάλα - literally 'steps' or 'stairs', usually the coastal village below.

Spilia / Σπηλιά = caves

Thermi / Θερμή = hot or warm

Thermopigi / Θερμοπηγή = thermal spring

Vathy / βαθύ, βαθύς = deep

Often there are inland villages with beach or harbour annexes just a few kilometres away. This dates back to the days when inland villages were safer havens and easier to protect from marauding pirates. With piracy a thing of the past, today's beach resort is often more developed and larger than the original inland village.

They may share the same name or a related name, with the village name ending changing to the genitive or possessive form, eg Eressos / Ερεσος (inland old village) and Skala Eressou / Σκάλα Ερεσού (beach village), Ano Gatzea / Ανω Γατζέα (upper Gatzea) and Kato Gatzea /Κάτω Γατζέα (lower Gatzea), although signposts and brochures will often adopt different spellings or forms, in the Greek or Latin letters, which can be confusing.

> **Did you know?**
> thermometer
> is a Greek word
> from
> **θερμός** = hot &
> **μέτρο** = measure

Language Difficulties

We all know how easy it is to get our Greek wrong and I'm sure the Greeks chuckle at many of our mistakes - here are a few from both sides.

The first two from **Gerry Brown**:

Kimolos did not have a 'self service' mini-market when Tony decided our self-catering meals needed spicing up. Off he went to the grocery shop to get some chilli powder. He came back with a box of candles.

Katerina was chalking her menu blackboard at the taverna, as usual with the help of a dog-eared Greek-English dictionary. Today's special was 'fishes balls'. After our giggling had subsided we told her that fish do not have balls. When we passed later that day the sign read 'fishes vaginas'!

* * *

*This sign was spotted and photographed in Lindos, Rhodes by **Ian Scoging**. He wasn't sure whether to go there to eat or if he would have to show his under garments conformed to local traditions!*

* * *

Terry Cocker had not been living in Greece long and was still getting to grips with a few basics in Greek. There were still jobs to do on the house when he went to the electrician to arrange for him to come in a week's time. When he got there he couldn't remember the word for 'week' or the day of the week, so with a mixture of words and sign language he asked Andonis to come to *"spiti mou, avrio, avrio, avrio, avrio, avrio, avrio, avrio"* - counting the days off on his fingers. Andonis laughed, *"Ah, mia evthomada; endaxi."* He got out his diary and wrote something on the appropriate day, AND he turned up on the right day. There is always more than one way to communicate in Greece!

> **Did you know?**
> **arithmetic**
> is a Greek word
> a direct import from the people who learnt much about calculating numbers
> η αριθμητική
> from **ο αριθμός** = number

This notice at the Aronis Taverna at Plaka beach, Naxos was spotted by **Marie Thérèse Magnan** of Rome. Unless it's a vegetarian taverna, does that really mean they serve things like rabbit stifado, pork souvlaki and goat chops from *'the own family'* ?

After a holiday encompassing Antiparos, Amorgos, Koufonissia, Schinoussa, Iraklia and Naxos, Marie Thérèse concluded "Greek Islands = Paradise."

* * *

John Sheppard Fidler told us of one possible advantage of having a daughter who has learnt good Greek. "Our younger daughter Isabel taught English for several years in Drama on the Greek mainland, enabling her to join us when we were on holiday in Thassos. She was by then a fluent Greek speaker. One evening we walked past the old harbour to eat at Patriakis taverna in Limenas, but when we arrived there were no tables available on the terrace. Patriakis asked Isabel if we would sit and have a drink by the entrance until one became free. Soon a waiter signalled that a table was ready and as he led us towards it he passed another waiter and said something to him out of the corner of his mouth. When we were seated I asked Isabel what he had said. Apparently he was just warning his colleague - *The lady speaks Greek!*"

I say, I say, I say ...

Greek Jokes - Reading & Translation Practice

Good Greek pronunciation is fundamental to being understood by Greek people. Practise reading these out loud. They will help your pronunciation and improve your colloquial word power when you translate them - and hopefully you will have a chuckle too.

- Καπνίζεις;
- Όχι, δεν καπνίζω.
- Πίνεις;
- Όχι, δεν πίνω.

    - Παίζεις χαρτιά;
    - Όχι.
    - Πηγαίνεις στο καφενείο;
    - Όχι.
- Και τότε τι κάνεις;
- Λέω ψέματα!

Ο ασθενής προς τον ψυχίατρο.

"Γιατρέ δεν είμαι καλά. Πολλές φορές ακούω φωνές χωρίς να βλέπω κανένα."

"Και πότε σας συμβαίνει αυτό;"

" Όταν τηλεφωνώ."

* * *

- Κύριε, είμαι ερωτευμένος με την κόρη σας, και ζητώ το χέρι της.
- Δεν έχω αντίρρηση εγώ, είδατε όμως και τη μητέρα της.
- Την είδα, αλλά προτιμώ την κόρη.

* * *

Ένας κύριος μπήκε στην μπουτίκ και είπε στην πωλήτρια:
- Θέλω ν'αγοράσω ένα πολύ όμορφο φόρεμα για τη γυναίκα μου.
- Τι σχέδιο προτιμάτε;
- Οποιοδήποτε.
- Τι χρώμα;
- Δε με νοιάζει.
- Τι ύφασμα;
- Όποιο νάναι.
- Το μέγεθος;
- Μου είναι αδιάφορο. Έτσι κι αλλιώς ότι και να της πάρω,
        θάρθει αύριο για να τ'αλλάξει.

Greek Language - Jokes to Read & Translate

"Καταδικάζεσαι σε πρόστιμο διακοσίων χιλιάδων δραχμών για εξύβριση δημοσίου προσώπου" λέει ο δικαστής στον κατηγορούμενο. "Θέλεις να πεις κάτι ;"
"Θα θελα κύριε δικαστά, αλλά οι τιμές σας είναι πολύ ακριβές."

* * *

Μια φορά έκαναν έρευνα για να εξακριβώσουν πως προτιμούν οι άντρες να ντύνονται οι γυναικες τους. Η απάντησις που έδωσε το μεγαλύτερο ποσοστό ήταν - πιο γρήγορα!

* * *

"Με συγχωρείς," λέει ο επιβάτης στην αεροσυνοδό, "πόσο ύψος έχει το αεροπλάνο;"
"Τρεις χιλιάδες μέτρα."
"Και πόσο πλάτος;"

"Θα είμαι ειλικρινής μαζι σου, νεαρέ," είπε ο πατέρας, "δεν είσαι σε θεση να ζήσεις την κόρη μου, αλλά αυτό δεν νομίζω οτι είναι πρόβλημα γιατί ούτε κι'εγώ είμαι!"

* * *

- Γιατρέ μου, το δεξί μου πόδι με τρελλαίνει στους πόνους.

- Μην ανησυχείς. Της ηλικίας ειναι.

- Δεν νομίζω, γιατρέ. Και το αριστερό μου πόδι έχει την ίδια ηλικία, αλλα δεν με πονάει καθόλου.

"Δεν είδες ότι το φως ήταν κόκκινο;" λέει ο αστυνομικός στον οδηγό που σταμάτησε.
"Το φως το είδα ότι ήταν κόκκινο" λέει ο οδηγός, "Εσάς όμως δεν είδα."

*Jokes supplied, advice and Greek text checked by **Antoine Bohdjalian***

Events

Olympic Games in Athens 2004

The Olympic Games are coming home!

The first Olympic Games were held in the Western Peloponnese in 776 BC and then every 4 years for more than a thousand years, until the Roman Emperor Theodosius 1 abolished them in 394 AD for being a 'pagan ritual'.

In ancient times there was an Olympic Truce when all hostilities between Greek city-states were suspended to allow everyone free passage to and from the games and a chance to compete in peace and friendship. In 1896 when the modern Olympic Games were held first in Athens, that Olympic Spirit was revived and, in spite of some problems in more recent history, that spirit is still the essence of the Olympic Games - with people coming together in friendship and competing not for reward but for honour and the joy of participating.

The ultimate accolade for the ancient competitors was to win the victor's crown (a wreath of laurel) - but they would return to their city states as heroes and benefit from gifts and honours from the city and its statesmen. Today's victors receive gold, silver and bronze medals, but from the faces of the winners communicated to millions all around the world you can see that pride in winning for their country is just as important as it ever was.

Preparations

Athens started preparing to be the venue for the 2004 Olympic Games even before winning the bid in September 1997. It was known that as the smallest country ever to host the Summer Olympic Games, in an area where traffic was becoming an increasing problem, that a modern transport infrastructure was needed to cope with the huge numbers of people - athletes, trainers, organisers, staff and volunteers as well as the many spectators who will descend on the host city.

An estimated crowd of 100,000 gathered to watch the first modern Olympic Games in 1896. On Sunday 22nd August 2004, the busiest day of the 2004 Olympics, Athens expects 400,000 spectators plus athletes, staff and the media to be moving around Athens' 15 sports locations. Not only transport, but hospitals, mobile medical units, security, communications and services catering to the needs of all, must be ready to cope.

Athens new airport opened at Spata, 27 kms east of Athens in March 2001 and is ramping up to receive and despatch more and more passengers, with advanced security systems to handle smooth access for visitors from around the world. Two new Metro lines have opened and further extensions will help to minimise road traffic and speed movement around the city. Upgraded old railway lines, a new tramway and new 32 km suburban railway line linking the Metro with the International airport will all help. 117 kilometres of new roads are being built, existing roads are being upgraded, more parking facilities created, some public places are being redesigned with many trees planted to create a greener Athens.

Fifteen sports venues will be built or upgraded from existing facilities. An entire Olympic village, more of a town really, is being built north of Athens to house 11,000 athletes from around the world with their 5,000 trainers, other associates and staff - no mean feat. Hotels and tour operators are gearing up to house the additional visitors, including the provision of 3 kms docking space at Piraeus for cruise ships to stay during the games.

After a slow start and initial teething troubles (even the Greeks struggle with their own bureaucracy), the organisers are back on track setting up the infrastructure to stage a successful Olympic Games in Athens 2004.

Events and Venues

The main sporting events run from the opening ceremony on 13th August to 29th August 2004 at 15 venues, mostly around Athens. Football events start 2 days earlier in Athens, Patras, Thessaloniki, Volos and Heraklion.

Before the games begin, the traditional journey of the **Olympic Torch** starts at ancient Olympia, as it has since the Berlin Olympics in 1936. Its flame burns continuously as runners take it around the world before arriving at the main stadium of the host city at the opening ceremony - this time back in Greece - where it continues burning until the closing ceremony. For the first

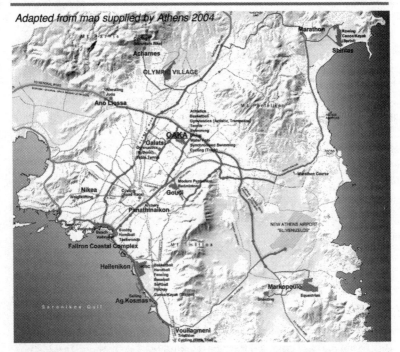

time the flame will visit all five continents represented by the five coloured interlocking circles of the Olympic emblem, and more countries than ever before. (Africa and South America were not included previously.)

The grand opening and closing ceremonies will be held at the centrepiece Athens Olympic Sports Complex (known locally as **OAKA**) at Maroussi, a northern suburb of Athens. The site is undergoing major redesign and upgrade for the games. Tennis, gymnastics, athletics, indoor games, swimming, diving, water polo and cycling events will take place at OAKA.

In addition to football stadia mentioned earlier, Athens' venues/events are:

The Faliron Coastal Complex near Piraeus for volley ball, hand ball, taekwondo, boxing. Nearby **Aghios Kosmas** is the centre for sailing.

Hellinikon Olympic Complex south of Athens for baseball, softball, hockey, fencing, basketball preliminaries and canoe events.

Marathon will of course be the starting point, as in ancient times, for its namesake race. Rowing and canoeing events will be held at nearby **Schinias**.

Goudi, northeast Athens, will host the modern pentathlon and badminton.

The 1896 games were held at **Panathinaikon** in the centre of Athens, which plays its part again for the finish of the marathon race and for archery.

Athens City Centre will be used for the road cycling events and **Acharnes** north of the Olympic village for mountain biking.

Vouliagmeni on south Attica coast for triathlon and cycling road race trials.

The **Markopoulo Olympic Equestrian Centre** is just south of the new Athens airport and east of the nearby **Markopoulo Shooting Centre**.

The **Nikea Weightlifting Hall** is southwest of Athens.

Wrestling and judo events will be at **Ano Liossa** northwest of Athens and **Galatsi**, a suburb in northwest Athens, will host table tennis and the rhythmic gymnastic events.

If you want to watch any of the events, or to know more about the Olympic Games you will find the latest details on their website www.athens.olympic.org. Tickets should start to be released 18 months before the start of the games. Not everyone can be there, but you can be sure that the events will be relayed to viewers in all parts of the world (220 countries) through the sophisticated information and telecommunications systems being made available to Press and Broadcasting Media.

The symbol chosen for the Athens 2004 Games is a white olive wreath on a blue background, like the traditional victor's crown, but also a symbol of peace and of the city of Athens. The Olympics 2004 mascots Athina and Fivos are modelled on an ancient Greek doll dating from 7th c. BC.

AΘHNA 2004

Aθηνά Φοίβος

Other Olympic Events

A four year **Cultural Olympiad** is taking place 2001-2004 promoting the artistic and cultural excellence of Greece - as poetry, music and sculpture displays were a part of the religious festivals from which the Olympics derived. Museums are being built and renovated, archaeological sites developed, artistic events, concerts, awards and seminars are happening in Greece and around the world promoting Greek culture. See www.cultural-olympiad.gr for more information.

The **Paralympic Games** will also be held in Athens, 17th - 28th September 2004, using many of the same facilities for the 4,000 athletes expected and coping with their special needs.

Whether you join the live spectators, watch from home or holiday or just travel to Athens at some other time - you will benefit from the planning and work that has gone into making the Athens 2004 Olympics a *unique* event.

Public Holidays in Greece - 2003 to 2005

On Public Holidays listed below you will find banks and public offices shut, but tourist services tend to stay open 7 days a week. One exception to this may be Easter Sunday when there are very few places open. Shops in towns and villages are shut by law on Sundays. Most dates below are the same in subsequent years, but those marked separately for 2004 ανδ 205 are moveable feasts, tied to the Greek Orthodox Easter dates (based on a different calculation to our Easter dates).

	Year 2003	Year 2004	Year 2005
New Year's Day	1st January		
Epiphany	6th January		
Ash Monday	10th March	23rd Feb	14th Mar
Independence Day	25th March		
Good Friday	25th April	9th Apr	29th Apr
Easter Sunday	27th April	11th Apr	1st May
Easter Monday	28th April	12th Apr	2nd May
Labour Day	1st May		
Pentecost	16th June	30th May	19th Jun
Whit Monday	17th June	31st May	20th Jun
Assumption Day	15th August		
Ochi Day	28th October		
Christmas Day	25th December		
Second Day of Christmas	26th December		

In addition to the above public holidays there will be local festivals commemorating local events or, more often, the name day of the patron saint of the local church. If you see festivities in progress, do ask around. You will often be encouraged to join in.

Greek Events in Britain

Most Greek Events in UK - concerts, exhibitions, etc - are not planned very far in advance, making it difficult to include information in this book. However we can give some useful contacts from whom you should be able to find out more.

The Hellenic Centre - 16-18 Paddington Street, London W1M 4AS Tel. 020 7487 5060 - Art exhibitions, talks, concerts, etc for members and non-members. The Hellenic Centre is also a useful source of information for other Greek events which are often notified to them.

Greece in Britain Events - Information from Cultural Office, London Greek Embassy, 1a Holland Park, London W11 3TP Tel 020 7727 3029

Trehantiri for Concert tickets - Greek pop, traditional and classical (p174)

Greek Films - Riverside Studios, Hammersmith Tel. 020 8237 1111

London South Bank - Concerts Box Office - Tel. 020 7960 4242

Book Reviews

Gates of the Wind by Michael Carroll

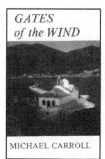

Publisher: Efstathiadis* ISBN 960 226 089 0 £4.50

The Northern Sporades islands are known as the 'Gates of the Wind' by local fishermen. This is Michael Carroll's personal story of the years he spent in the area, initially on his sailing boat *Astarte*, then putting down roots and building a house in a quiet bay in Skopelos. He incorporates many interesting details about the islands of the Sporades in a very readable way, but more tellingly relates incidents with the local people he meets, particularly Vangeli who befriends and guides him.

Alexander at the World's End by Tom Holt

Publisher: Abacus, ISBN 0-349-11315-7 £7.99 (€15.36 paid in Greece).

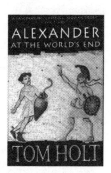

A follow up to the much enjoyed The Walled Orchard, this book relates the story of life in the Hellenic World at the time of Alexander the Great through the eyes of a cynical Athenian philosopher, the grandson of the comedy writer raconteur of the previous novel. His path crosses Alexander's in a way that influences both of their lives and maybe changes the course of history. Good fun and an insight to life in ancient Greece.

It's All Greek to Me by Ann Hill Workman

Publisher: Efstathiadis* ISBN 960 226 548 5 £3.99

With the prospect of retirement and a modest pension ahead, Ann and her husband Ian decide to set out on an 'oldies Odyssey' to spend a little time exploring their favourite country, Greece, and to live a little (on a budget) before they really are 'over the hill'. She relates their experiences in Crete, starting out from Chania, enjoying their adventure as a mature couple. Entertaining and fun.

Greek Wines - A Comprehensive Guide by Geoff Adams

Publisher: Winemaster Publishing,
ISBN 0-95420-330-5 £ 7.99 from Gazelle*

This book is an excellent guide with a non-stuffy approach to over 460 Greek wines from 75 wine producers. Not being wine connoisseurs, but enjoying more than the odd bottle of cheap wine as well as occasionally appreciating the quality of more expensive wines, it was good to see so many of the wines regularly encountered in tavernas and supermarket shelves in Greece and the UK. Recognising the tasting descriptions and ratings of those we know gives confidence in the descriptions of others to try. Included are guides to Greek vine-growing regions, Greek grapes, vintages, wine classifications, UK Greek wine retailers and a glossary to help you understand some of the tasting and other terms used.

Only the Best, Greek Cooking Reinvented by Maria Haramis

Publisher: Axon Publications SA ISBN 960-377-055-8 £8.99

An unusual cookery book with no sign of moussaka or many of the standards you would expect from a Greek cook book. A kind of Greek Nouvelle Cuisine (Νέο μαγειρική?) in that it aims to provide recipes for a more healthy diet for our waistlines and arteries, but it sticks with traditional Greek ingredients, even offering several recipes using trahana, the mainstay of many a Greek peasant's winter fare for centuries. Between the Festive Bread, Fisherman's Soup and Mrs Haritoulas' Custard Pie are more glamourous dishes Quail with Cherries, Potato skins with Botargo (pressed grey mullet roe - the Beluga caviar of Greece) and Rose Petal Sorbet. The recipes - about 56 - are mostly uncomplicated, but you may have difficulty finding ingredients for some. Certainly this book offers new ways with Greek food.

Charming Small Hotels & Restaurants, Greece by Robin Gauldie

Publisher: Duncan Petersen Publishing
ISBN 1 903301 21 1 £10.99

For those who prefer small hotels and guesthouses with a genuine personal welcome, this illustrated 210 page guide suggests a few in most parts of Greece. Some areas are better represented than others - the central mainland and Pelion, some of the Cyclades and Sporades islands, but there are few in the north Aegean or north east mainland and very few restaurants were included in spite of the title (a separate index might have helped to identify them). Many of the hotels are in charming renovated old buildings, most are away from the modern tourist jungles. The price guidelines show the majority are more expensive than most travellers to Greece would expect - but there are some more reasonably priced gems amongst them. The selection criteria are admirable for any discerning Grecophile and the descriptions and colour pictures are mouthwatering. If you pick an area well represented you could easily prearrange a quite exceptional touring holiday from this guide.

Trees & Shrubs of Greece by George Sifkas

Publisher: Efstathiadis* ISBN 960 226 593 0 £14.50

This new edition revised Dec 2001, includes 203 varieties of trees and shrubs to be found in Greece, illustrated with over 400 colour photographs and sketches to help you identify them. Only a few thousand years ago Greece was covered with vast forests although the climate was not so different then to now. Today's species are still the same, but deforestation, although now illegal, is still a problem. Fortunately the Greek species are strong and forests are spreading in parts of the mountains no longer inhabited. George Sifkas' descriptions are clear and with the help of close-up pictures and sketches of specific features, an explanation of each 'genus' (family) of plants, leaf identification and flower and fruit parts explained you will find this book a useful aide to recognising the trees and shrubs you see on your travels in Greece.

Rough Guide to Greece (Mainland and Islands)

Publisher: Rough Guides ISBN 1 85828 866 5 £13.99 Greece

Latest editions of the above and The Greek *Islands* Rough Guide (Feb 2002) seem to share much of the same text, so unless you are not interested in the mainland (which does not have its own Guide) you should get the 1140 page ALL Greece guide. (Islands Guide appx 650 pages, £11.99). The new guides include a colour front section and a clearer 2 colour layout throughout. The background sections, descriptions of areas and places of interest are helpful based on continuing research, but not all sections are updated. Resort specifics (hotels, tavernas) tend to be 'telling it like it was on the day the researcher was last there'. Allowing for personal opinions you may not agree with, Rough Guides are still one of the best guides to Greece.

The Archaeology of Ancient Greece by James Whitley

Publisher: Cambridge University Press P/back ISBN 0 521 62733 8 £21.95
Hardback ISBN 0 521 62205 0 £60

This 484 page illustrated tome is for the real enthusiasts, using up to date research and findings to explain the Archaic to Classical periods of Greece (1000 - 300BC). The author explains in readable text how the material evidence found can be used to answer historical and cultural questions about the lives of the ancient Greeks. The illustrations - photographs, sketches and plans, are clear although sometimes separated from the relevant text. Judging from the long pages of bibliography and James Whitley's credentials this is a well researched work as we would expect from the Cambridge University Press.

The Komboloi and its History by Aris Evangelinos

Publisher: Komboloi Museum, Nafplio ISBN960-86271-1-7 €9 in Greece, may not be available UK.

The book tells the story of Aris Evangelinos' quest. Fired by tales from his grandfather, he sets out to find the origins and symbolism of the komboloi. Along the journey, which includes Asia and the deserts of Africa, he meets many diverse people from whom he builds a fascinating and sometimes surreal story of how and when 'the beads' have been used and their purpose in other cultures.

The Other Greece Η άλλη Ελλάδα by Costas Vasilakis

Publisher: Livani ISBN 960-14-0484-8 £35 from Gazelle*

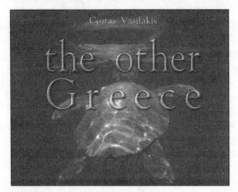

This is a beautifully produced glossy 'coffee table' book - 242 large pages full of colour photographs of the Greece that few tourists see, but many of us would like to. They are sensual pictures of landscapes and nature taken by 24 photographers in 180 different (very different) areas of Greece. In the prologue Costas Vasilakis says *"To-day's city dweller needs to re-discover nature... to escape from the artificial environment which he himself has created."* This book does just that - it is a wonderful journey, where you can drool over the sights and sensations of the 'other' real Greece.

Previous reviews by Sylvia Cook, the following recommendation from Jenny Booth:

The Potters House by Rosie White

Publisher: Arrow ISBN 0099 27157 paperback £6.99

This story of life during the winter months following an earthquake and tidal wave is set on a fictitious island, Halemni, not far from the Turkish coast and Rhodes. It is not a disaster story as such, focusing more on the relationships between various people. As most of the novels set in Greece that I read have been set in the 'spring to autumn' period, it was interesting to read about life after the visitors have gone home.

Greek Music

Rebetika & Laïka *by Chris Williams*

*Chris, who plays several traditional Greek instruments, writes for Folk Roots maga-
zine and lectures on music, has been writing regular articles for our Greek-o-File
music slot since June 2000. Here he explains two of the styles of Greek music you
will come across today with recommendations for representative music from Trehantiri,
London's Greek music shop.*

Anyone coming to Greek music for the first time will pretty soon come across
two new terms, **Rebetika** (sometimes written as *Rembetika*) and **Laïka**.
Each of these represents a whole world of music, but in this article I will try
to sketch out some of the essentials.

Rebetika

The term *Rebetika* (or *Rebetika tragoudia*, *Rebetika songs*) is usually used
to refer to the songs of the urban subculture of Athens and Piraeus in the
years following the influx of Greek refugees from Turkey in the 1920s. This
is as much a sociological as a musical phenomenon, and the lyrics that are
integral to the songs deal in a raw, uncompromising and sometimes shock-
ing manner with subjects such as drugs, crime and violence.

In fact, the roots of the *Rebetika* predate the 1920s slums of Athens and
Piraeus with which this music is associated. These roots are to be found in
the cafe music of the Greek communities of Western Turkey, especially in
Smyrna and Constantinople, and the social antecedents are to be found in
the large Greek urban centres of the late 19th and early 20th centuries. For
all the toughness of their lyrics musicians such as Yovan Tsaous were highly
accomplished, and some may even have performed classical music in Constantinople prior to their emigration to Greece. Although the *Rebetika* are
rightly seen as inseparably linked to the development of the bouzouki, recordings feature many other instruments, including the miniature bouzouki
known as *baglamas* as well as the *tambouras* lute.

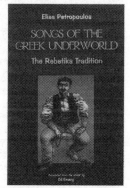

The *Rebetika* constitute a rich and fascinating musical universe with far deeper roots in broader
Greek culture than can be covered here. Anyone
interested in learning more should start by reading **Songs of The Greek Underworld by Elias
Petropoulos** (translated Ed Emery, Saqi Books
ISBN 0 86356 368 6 - £12.95).

There are many compilations of Rebetika, the best
being those in the original style with no electri-
cally assisted instrumentation. Try one 'cleaned
up' from original recordings on old 78s from FM's
The Greek Archives Series -Vol. 5 **Songs of the**

Underground (FM 631 £13.99) which includes a booklet, mostly in Greek, but with a useful English section explaining each song.

Another suggestion is a more recent recording of a traditional Rebetika band including Giorgos Tzortzis and Nikolas Syros - The band and the CD are called **'To Palio Mas Spiti' - Our Old Home** (Motivo NM1058 £15.99).

Laïka

If the *Rebetika* constitute a large but relatively well-defined entity, *Laïka* is a much looser term. *Laïka tragoudia* means, literally 'popular songs', and the phrase in its current sense seems first to have been applied to a kind of commercially produced pop song that first appeared in the 1950s. These songs are hard-edged but impassioned and, for me, found their true voice in the 1960s with the singer **Stelios Kazantzidis**. They rely heavily on 'oriental' scale types and, because of the passionate and often fatalistic lyrical content, are often seen as the heir to the *Rebetika* tradition. However, equally important to the success of the genre were the Western commercial production and promotional values which propelled it, and the increasing use of Western-style instrumentation in the form of drum kits, electric bass, keyboards and, above all, amplification; this was never a genre for purists.

As with the *Rebetika*, the bouzouki (suitably electrified) is central to the *Laïka*, and standards of performance have always been at virtuoso level. Although the term *Laïka* seems at times to be applied to quite different kinds of music the important thing is that the *Laïka* are to be distinguished from Greek folk song (*dhimotika)* the art songs (*entechna tragoudia*) of a composer such as Manos Hadzidakis.

Although not a high-status genre (at least not in the early days), the *Laïka* have attracted some excellent musicians and vocalists. Since the 1950s and 60s there has been a softening of some of the harder edges of the

Laïka, and it is probably more useful to talk of a sub-genre that would include artists such as **Yiorgos Dalaras**, **Viky Mosholiou**, **Haris Alexiou** and **Manolis Mitsias**. More recently **Eleftheria Arvanitaki** has incorporated some of the instrumentation and soundscape of less commercial music to create a distinctive new song type that is both popular and expressive of Greek culture more generally.

For the earlier *Laïka* search out anything by Stelios Kazantzidis - perhaps **Stelios Kazantzidis Sings** 24 hits (Minos 4801332 £15.99), or a collection of his homeland Northern Greece Songs, **Ta Pontiaka** (MBI 10744 £15.99).

Any compilation of Dalaras recordings can also be recommended. For later developments try **Eleftheria Arvanitaki, *Stin Arhi tou Tragoudiou: I Megales Epityhies*** - *At the Beginning of the Song: Greatest Hits* (Lyra CD ML 4983).

Chris Williams plays Cretan lyra, laoto and other traditional Greek instruments in his group, Troia Nova. For information or bookings email Chris@williams001.fsnet.co.uk.

Editor's Tip

If you don't know what kind of Greek music or which artists you like, you could try sampling different styles by buying inexpensive CDs which come as 'free gifts' with Greek music magazines such as **Δίφωνο**, or you can often find 3 or 4 old re-releases and compilations packed together with a poster book in Greek newsagents. Δίφωνο CDs are usually good quality - we found an excellent one of the film music of Xarharkos and another Eleftheria sampler (Δίφωνο is available from Trehantiri, at £5.50 UK price).

In Greece we recently bought 4 *Laïka* CDs with a poster book for about €12 all really enjoyable. It introduced us to new favourites - **Tolis Voskopoulos** (like a Greek Charles Aznavour) and **Marinella** (gorgeous sultry voice), so was exceptional value. There are many CDs by these two currently available, try **Tolis Voskopoulos Greatest Hits (Οι Μεγαλύτερες Επιτυχίες Του)** 20 tracks from 1969-1999, Minos 5-29703-2 £15.99.

Useful Websites

www.greekofile.co.uk, our own website, is designed for marketing Greek-o-File products, but also has a number of links to other useful sites. Jenny Booth wrote to us : *"I recommended your web site to someone recently and looked at it again myself. The links through to other sites of interest are great and I spent some valuable surfing time learning how good olive oil and Metaxa are for me! Also found lots of information on Kalymnos, our next destination."*

www.aia.gr - Athens International Airport site inc. departures/arrivals times.

www.all-hotels.gr - not all but many Greek hotels listed with classification.

www.athensnews.gr - Greece's English weekly news, inc. classified ads.

www.culture.gr - Greek Ministry of Culture site, events information, etc.

www.geocities.com/HotSprings/1794/greekgde.html - Cap'n Barefoot's naturists' guide to Greek beaches.

www.gnto.gr - Greek National Tourism Organisation.

www.gogreece.com - Internet Guide to Greece.

www.greece.gr - Government sponsored information site about Greece.

www.greekembassy.org.uk - London Greek Embassy and Consulate site.

www.greekislandhopping.com - Frewin Poffley's support site for readers of the Greek Island Hopping Guide, latestupdates.

www.greekproducts.com - shopping and information site

www.greektravel.com - information on places to go and contacts in Greece.

www.gtpweb.com - Greek Travel Pages' latest ferry schedules, travel agents.

www.hellasworld.co.uk - an enthusiast's site - info on culture, travel, etc.

www.hri.org - Hellenic Resources Network - news and information.

www.kypros.org/greek/cgi-bin/lexicon - English/Greek dictionary, part of Greek Lessons site being revised as we go to print.

www.learndirect.co.uk - to find local or correspondence Greek classes.

www.magicaljourneys.com - travel information on all parts of Greece.

www.protoselida.com/english - The Greek Front Page links to many sites.

www.speak-greek.co.uk - enthusiasts site to share tips, contacts, etc.

www.tranexp.com:2000 - translation to/from Greek - words or sentences up to 25 words.

weather.yahoo.com/regional/GRXX.html, or **www.robby.gr/weather.**

Short Story

Liverpool, Southampton, Falmouth ... *by Sylvia Cook*

"Poso Kani?" she asked hesitantly as she held up the can of Fanta orange, taken from his fridge. to show the man in the periptero (street kiosk). He replied, quickly and in Greek. She didn't understand a word!

She smiled and held out a note, *"How much?"* He smiled back, *"From England?"* he asked. *"Nai"* (Yes). *"Ah, Liverpool, Southampton, Falmouth, Swansea, Immingham..."* He listed the ports he had been to in Britain. She remembered hearing a similar list before from a sailor in Corfu.

"Where you from?" he enquired. *"Exeter, it's in the south west of England"* she told him.

He spoke fairly good English - certainly better than her pathetic attempts at Greek. She'd swatted up from Greek language tapes and books in the weeks prior to this trip, hoping to be able to communicate in Greek - but now she reverted to English. It was easier. She paid and went to her spot in the shade to sip her cooling drink and perhaps read a bit.

Katrina had arrived on the island only yesterday - with nearly a month in Greece ahead of her, this was just the start of an adventure that would take her she knew not where. She'd been to Greece before on a package holiday to Corfu with her (now ex-) husband Mike. She'd loved the friendliness of the Greeks, their natural hospitality, the way the village people enjoyed the simple things of life. Mike had wanted only to stay by their hotel pool and in the evenings drink and get drunk with English people. She'd tried to learn a little Greek that time. Mike said *"Why bother?, They all speak English here."* But even in the busy resort they had appreciated her efforts at Greek.

The day she'd booked them to go on a trip around the island, stopping off at an inland village, then on to Paleokastritsa and back via the olive groves and leafy lanes, Mike had been too hung over from the night before and didn't feel like it, so she'd gone anyway, without him. She talked briefly with some of the couples on the trip, but also enjoyed her own company, especially wandering round the streets in the little village they'd stopped at.

Seeing her looking around, one little old lady had beckoned her into her house. It was just two rooms. The first had two enormous wine barrels at one end taking up half the space. The other half had a small wooden couch with a stripey colourful rug over, a small table next to the modern refrigerator and cooker, a cupboard with lace mat on top and some framed photographs. Without a common language the lady explained that the barrels were for wine and would be filled again in September. The pictures included an old, now sepia-coloured photograph of her with her husband on their wedding day, another of her husband as a young man in the navy - strikingly handsome, now sadly no longer with her. Another much newer photograph was of her son now in the army on his National Service. The second room had her simple bed, a rug on the floor and just one cupboard.

It was a hot day. The lady offered her a glass of cold water on a lace covered tray with a small plate of sesame topped biscuits and insisted, though she tried to refuse, that she eat some (they were quite tasty, actually) - and when she would not take another, it was wrapped up in a paper serviette and pressed in her hand to take with her. This simple house and the lady's simple life where she took the best things from the modern world, but seemed content to live an uncluttered existence, made a lasting impression on Katrina. Mike didn't understand when she tried to tell him how moved she had been to be invited into the lady's home.

Anyway Mike was history now. They had been a couple since they met at college and probably got married out of habit. He was a computer programmer, she now a primary school teacher. They had always assumed they would have children one day, but had not been in a hurry, preferring to wait until they had a better house, then a better car - then they had grown apart and she was glad they had not got round to it.

Her mother had brought her up on her own until she was about 7, before meeting and marrying Harry. She knew it hadn't been easy for mum. With the responsibility of a young daughter and problems finding child-minders, mum had mostly worked in hotels or bars before meeting Harry. They'd lived with granny and grandad in their new house in Taunton for a couple of years after she was born, but she knew they were always rowing. Mum and she had moved out and gone back to be near Falmouth where mum had lived as a youngster. They had a good life together and were friends as well as mother and daughter, but mum never said anything about her real father. Harry was OK, if a bit boring. She called Harry 'Dad', but her two younger half brothers had always been closer to him. She was mummy's girl! Then suddenly last year Harry had a heart attack - he was only in his late 50's. Now mum was alone again, like her really.

Lots of friends had been surprised when she'd said she was going to Greece alone for 4 weeks. She'd organised a return flight, but nothing else and was going to wander round some islands, finding rooms as she went, anything basic would do. Her mum had understood, but said to take care and watch out for the Greek romeos! But she was not looking for a man. She'd had enough of them for a while.

On the beach that first day she looked again at her Greek language book. Next day back at the periptero she picked up a can and offered the correct money. She said *"Kali mera, ti kanetai?"* (Good morning, how are you?) to the old sailor inside. *"Kala, kai esis?"* (Well, and you?) the man asked back. *"Poli kala. Einai mia poli orea mera"* (Very well. It is a beautiful day.) she replied. *"Bravo, bravo!"* (Well done, well done!). *"Pos s'elena?"* (What is your name?) he asked. *"Katrina"* she replied. *"Ah, Katerina. It was my mother's name."* Most Greek people changed her name to their more common Katerina, but she quite liked it. *"Kai esis, Pos s'elena?"* she asked him. *"Yiorgos, but you can call me George." "Can't I call you Yiorgo?" "Of course you can."*

Life was good. Yesterday she had done very little, just letting the stress of the previous months melt away in the Greek sunshine, gazing out over the blue, blue sea and in the evening watching the sun go down behind the rock, colouring the cliffs opposite a magnificent fiery orange and filling the sky with gold before disappearing - knowing it would be back again the next day. Today she would look around the town, wander round the tourist shops and up into the back streets to see a little of Greek life and maybe go to the ancient ruins nearby that she had read about in her guide book.

She loved this place. She felt at home and relaxed here. It was quintessentially Greece - blue skies, misty horizon fading into the dark blue sea, white sugar cube houses clustered round the harbour and up the hillside, Greek music wafting from shady tavernas, old men sat outside kafeneions, old ladies sat on their steps gossiping. Yes, there were tourists too, but not too many as the ferry only came here two or three times a week and that tended to put the crowds and mass-market tour operators off.

She had found a room easily, being approached at the port when she got off the ferry, together with Sue and John, a couple in their 50's whom she'd met on the ferry. They were old hands at Greek island hopping. At first Katrina had been a little apprehensive, but they had assured her that there was always somewhere to stay -*"just don't commit yourself until you've seen the room and haggle on the price, or say no if you think it's too much, but just accept if it's a good deal"* they said.

Their bags were put in the back of a three wheeled green truck. John got in the back with the luggage, sat on a white plastic chair by the side rail. She squeezed in with Sue and the driver as they were taken up the hill, not far, to a small block of 6 rooms, 3 up, 3 down, surrounded by flowers and fruit trees and with amazing views over the small 'Horio' and port to one side and to a quiet sandy bay backed by cliffs and a rocky promontory the other side. With Sue and John doing the haggling it had been easy. She took their advice not to try to see too much and with plenty of time in hand decided to stay here at least 5 days before moving on, but not to commit herself in case she wanted to stay longer. This was Katrina's idea of paradise.

It was *misi-meri* (lunchtime) when she suddenly felt in need of a little food and a drink, but she was at the top of the village where there did not seem to be many tavernas. There was one men's bar, where a tourist couple and 6 or 7 Greek men were sat, so she sat outside too. When the owner eventually emerged from the cool dark interior she asked for a beer and *"Eketai tipota na famai?"* (Do you have anything to eat?). He replied very fast in Greek and she did not understand. It was Yiorgos who came to her aid. She had not recognised the man from periptero when she sat down as he'd had his back to her. *"Ah Yiorgo"* she was pleased to see his friendly smiling face. He explained this was an ouzerie and if she just wanted a little to eat the owner would bring some 'mezes' - bits and pieces of whatever he had to accompany the drinks. *"That sounds great"*, she said. Yiorgos ordered.

He adjusted his seat a little and put the small round table in front of her alongside the one he shared with two other men. She was happy to join them. Yiorgos was a gentle man and a gentleman.

They were drinking ouzo with water and obviously having a good chin-wag and putting the world to rights. A small plate of feta cheese, drizzled with olive oil and sprinkled with oregano, with some bread arrived, but not the beer. Just a small ouzo bottle and another glass into which Yiorgo poured ouzo from the little bottle. He passed it to her with the water jug. Well, what the heck. Why not? She filled her glass to the top with water, watching the clear liquid turn milky white while Yiorgo topped up the other glasses then banged his glass on the table with a *"Yammas"*, she clinked hers against his, and the other two men leaned over to clink her glass and each other's too. *"Yammas"* they all said.

Yiorgos introduced her. *"Katerina, this is Kostas - 85 years old and he still works on his farm, and this is Dimitris, he was on ships too. Katerina is from England."* *"Southampton, Glasgow, Liverpool, Immingham..."* Dimitris listed the ports he had been to. She laughed and said *"They all do that"*. Another small plate arrived, this time with wedges of peeled cucumber. They all clinked glasses and said *"Yammas"* again. She tried to sip hers slowly, at least all this *'yammas'*ing every time a glass was picked up helped slow down the drinking pace, and she tucked in as more small plates of delicacies arrived - tiny fish in oil, tsatsiki, dark wine coloured olives, sun ripened tomato cut into chunks, a yellow cheese (paler than cheddar, but similar texture), beans in tomato sauce (not baked beans, but delicious giant beans in a thick tasty sauce), always with small pieces of bread - and Dimitris ordered another little ouzo bottle, then Kostas.

Kostas did not speak English, but Yiorgos told Katrina that Kostas had 7 children and more than 20 grandchildren and now many great grandchildren too. She asked if he, Yiorgos, had any children. *"No"* Yiorgos said sadly. He'd never married. Having had a few ouzos by now Katrina cheekily asked, *"What, a good looking man like you? Why not?"*

"Ah there was one girl once. In England. We were in love. I could not love another as I loved her."

"Why didn't you marry then?"

"We were going to get married, but ..." and he paused, his face a picture of desolation, *"I lost her."*

"How could you 'lose' her if you were in love?"

"The life of a sailor is difficult. You don't always know where you will go and when you will be back. I could not marry her if I had no money, so I had to work hard to save for our home and our future; to save for the day when I would not be a sailor. We met many times in Falmouth, when we docked there. Then one year I broke my leg in a silly accident, so I was stuck on the island all winter and didn't get back on the same boat. My next boat did not go to Falmouth. I tried to write. I looked at all the books and tried to write in English to her to say I would come as soon as I could, and please wait for me. She did not answer. Maybe she did not get the letters. She did not know where my family lived because I was always at sea. She expected to see me after 3 months, but it was 2 years later I jumped ship in Southampton and found my way back there. She was gone. The place we used to meet had been pulled down and they were building new shops. The house she lived in with her family was sold to someone else and they said they did not know where the other people had gone. I lost her. ... There were other girls, yes, but... ", he paused again, for a long time, sighing *"no one like my Margarita."* He looked down.

He looked so dejected. The mood of the company had changed from jocularity to sadness as he reminisced. Katrina said nothing, awkwardly fingering the little gold pendant on the chain round her neck.

It was one of those small gold disks with an inscription in some ancient unknown script spiralling around, said to be a copy of something found on Crete. She had seen similar disks of all sizes in the tourist shops. Hers was older. It had been her mother's. When she was little she'd often played with the beads and baubles in her mum's jewellery box. She liked this little gold disk which had been on a flimsy chain which had broken. Around the time her mum, Margaret, had got married to Harry, she'd said Katrina could have it. It was something she was once given by someone very special and she'd like her to keep it. She'd only come across it again when sorting through personal things when Mike and she separated. It was almost a last minute impulse to put it on another chain to wear for this holiday in Greece.

Yiorgos looked up and seeing Katrina, smiled. *"You remind me of her. I gave her a disk just like that the last time we were together. We were so much in love and maybe got a bit carried away ... alone together one night"*!

Index of Advertisers

*Tour Operator advertisers are cross referenced in the **'Who Goes Where'** section (pages 64-69). Other advertisers are listed here.*

Index

*In this index main article subjects are in **bold,** reference only items in plain text and place names listed after the island or region name.*

*Main article subjects **bold**, reference only plain text, place names after island/region.*

*Main article subjects **bold**, reference only plain text, place names after island/region.*

*Main article subjects **bold**, reference only plain text, place names after island/region.*

Greek-o-File Magazine Issues

Greek-o-File started life at the end of 1998 as a quarterly publication available on annual subscription. We published 15 issues before changing to this book format to hopefully find a wider audience. The quarterlies were A4 size and punched to build into a FILE of information on all things Greek. Back issues are still available direct from Greek-o-File if there is something or somewhere you would like to know more about - or if you just can't get enough of reading about Greece and all things Greek.

Issues included front page article (mostly topical), letters, places to go, travel notes for shorter anecdotes, special features on all kinds of subjects, Greek life and traditions, food & cooking, history, mythology, Greek language, book reviews and music - in similar style to the articles in this book - average 28 A4 pages.

Many subscribers enthusiastically sent in contributions for consideration, or letters of appreciation or their news. Most just enjoyed reading about others' experiences.

Here are the main articles published in each issue:

INTRODUCTORY ISSUE
What is Greek-o-File?
Greek Map, Poet's Corner
Lesvos - Eressos & West Profile
Andros Profile
Driving to Greece
Food Introduction, Tsatsiki & Moussaka
The Greek Coffee Experience
Greek Feast Days & Holidays
When General Metaxas Said 'Okhi'
Who's Who in Mythology - The Gods
Introduction to Greek Language -
    Alphabet, Where is.. & Nouns
Book Reviews & Music Suggestions

Issue 1999/1
Tourism from UK
SE Peloponnese &
Tinos Profiles
Sleeping Under Stars
Cruising the Aegean
Food - Trachanas &
    Fassolatha
A Day in Village Life
The Election Poster
Pirates Carry off King's Daughter -
    History or Mythology
Mythological Creatures
Language - Greetings & Verbs

Issue 1999/2
Tour Operator or Independent Travel?
Rhodes & Syros
Buying a House in Greece
Walking in Zagoria
First Impressions of a Tourist to Greece
Food - Oregano
    & Chicken
Advice to
    Travellers
Understanding
    the Balkan
    Problem
Language -
    Directions &
    Nouns
Greek for
    Computers

Issue 1999/3
Island Hopping -
Piraeus, Kimolos
Paxos
Addicted to Greece
Poem - Foul Play
Food - Octopus &
  Courgettes
Traditions in
  Olympos, Karpathos
Spiros' New Roof
The Birth of Philosophy
Arion - The Boy on the Dolphin
Language - Numbers, Money, Verbs

Issue 1999/4
Earthquake Zone
West Peloponnese & Sifnos
DIY Greek Style
Animal Welfare
Greek Wines in UK
Sifniot Chick Pea
  Balls
The Magic of
  Greek Dance
My Other Half
Olympia & the Games,
Tantalus
Language - Link words,
  Pronouns

Issue 2000/1
Parthenon Marbles Going Home?
Milos & Karpathos Profiles

Klima, Milos

Notes - Kalymnos, Lefkas & Meganissi
Cretan Plant Life, Colours of Greece
Greece by Motor Cycle
Greek Easter & Easter Food
Museum of Archaeology,
Timetable of History, House of Atreus
Language - Past & Future, Greek Fable

Issue 2000/2
Athens Metro
Pelion
Naxos
Seeing Stars in
  Greece
Cheese Making
Tiropittakia
Greek People -
  Crete &
  Kalymnos
Rebirth of a
  Nation 1821-29
Centaurs - Barbarians or
  Ancient Lager Louts ?
Language - Introductions & Subjunctive
Ross Daly Music

Issue 2000/3
Forest Fires, Ferries
Corfu & Tilos Profiles
House Buying Update
Wines in Greece
The 'Exo Fournos', Stifado Recipe
Greek Name Days - I
Grecian Blues, Chairs
Golden Age of Greece
Dionysos - God of Wine & Revelry
Adjectives & 'What did you say?'
Cretan Dance Music

Corfu, Lefkimmi

Issue 2000/4

Athens New Airport
Igoumenitsa to Ioannina & Symi Profiles
Medical Experiences
Seven Crowded Months
Horta & Recipes
My House - At Last
Greek Name Days - 2
When Oracles Ruled
Advice for British Forces in Greece WW2
Irregular Verbs
Greek Ottoman Music

Folk Museum Melingi, nr Dodona

Issue 2001/1

End of the Drachma
Ithaki & Schinoussa Profiles
Athens to Kalamata by Train
Walking in Southern Pindos
The Photo Shoot, Sponge Diving
Raki & Tsipouro, Dolmades
Getting to Grips with Greek Transport
The Wall
Homer's
  Odysseus
Language - Food,
  Greeklish
Sifnos Poem
Yannis Parios

Issue 2001/2

Greek Ferries Update
Kefalonia & Halki Profiles
Travel Notes - Alonissos
Weddings in Greece, Words of Wisdom
Greek Yoghurt & Recipes
Greek Fishermen
Knights of
  St John
Legend of
  Narcissus
Positions &
  Adverbs
Bouzouki

*Filming of
Captain Corelli's
Mandolin*

Issue 2001/3

Noise Pollution in
  Modern Greece
Parga & Around
NW Crete
Cycladic
  Holidays
New Airport - The Reality
Driving in Greece
Greek Vegetables & Briam Recipe
Visiting Greek Churches
British Campaign 1940-1, The Muses
Language - Driving, Road & A Fable
Music Book & Dalaras

Issue 2001/4

Ancient Nemean Games

Samos & Meganissi Profiles
Notes - S. Peloponnese, Skiathos
Last of the Summer Retsina
Corfu Seasons
Fish & Recipes
Christmastime on Our Island
End of Minoan Civilisation
Minos & The Minotaur
Language - Time & More on Nouns
Music - Eleftheria Arvanitaki

Thassos, Sotiras village

Issue 2002/1

Winter News from Greece
Thassos, N.Corinth Gulf to Delphi
Notes - Search for War Grave, Saints be
 Praised! Psari Forada, Crete
Working In Greece
Land for Sale
Coping with Special Diets, Greek Salad
Hospitality
Sparta & Mystras Poems
Ancient Site of Delphi
Language - The Home & Adverbs
Traditional Music & Dance

Issue 2002/2

Visiting with Respect
Chios, Donoussa
Notes - Island Hopping, Marathias, Corfu
When Harry met Gwyn, Gill...
Mediterranean Monk Seals
Beers of Greece
Smyrna Soutzoukakia
The Greek Family, Chios Gum Mastic
Theophrastus
Orion, Unlucky in Love?
Language - The Body & Passive Verbs
Trihordo, Sound of Soul

<u>Greek-o-File Back Issues & other Purchases</u>

Back issues are available direct from Greek-o-File at
£4 for just one, or **just £3 each** for 2 or more inc UK P&P.

If you would like all 15 we will include a FREE 1.5" capacity Greek-o-<u>File</u>
(A4 white 4 ring binder with logo & set of dividers) for £45 - UK only.

Additional copies of this book are available direct for just **£8** each and future
volumes will also be available direct with free UK post and packing.
The Greek-o-File Volume 2 is planned for publication November 2003.

Overseas purchasers, additional costs for postage:

to Rest of EU - add 50p per issue, £1 per book
to Rest of World add £1 per issue, £2 per book
(Files not available for posting overseas - full set 15 for price of 14)

GIFTS - We can enclose a gift card with a short message from you,
despatched after cheque clearance or around a specified date - 2nd class post.

Payments by £ cheque, postal order or GBP International Money Order made out to
Greek-o-File and sent to 4 Harvey Road, Langley, Nr Slough, Berks SL3 8JB - or
contact Greek-o-File for bank details for direct transfer. (see form on p192)

Tel. 01753 544475, Fax 01753 544214 or email mail@greekofile.co.uk
or check on website www.greekofile.co.uk.

Prices valid at least to March 2004

Greek-o-File Offers

Acting as agents for **Ectaco UK Ltd**, Greek-o-File are pleased to offer 10%   off the retail price for **English/Greek** hand held **Electronic Translators**. Send cheque made payable to Greek-o-File. Call Greek-o-File or see Ectaco website www.electronicdictionary.co.uk for more details.

Greek & English Talking Translator & Dictionary,
EG2200T £175 retail **£157.50** inc VAT & UK P&P from Greek-o-File

Instant reverse translation, 450,000 words, phrases, English idioms translated, clear 4 line display, uses 3 AAA batteries. Originally designed for Greeks learning English, the 2-way features of the above model make it very useful for helping you to learn and communicate in Greek too AND it's fun to use!

Are you paying too much for your travel insurance ?

We've used **Columbus Direct** Travel Insurance personally for years and are pleased that Columbus are offering **Greek-o-File contacts** 10% discount off their already **low rates**

Europe - Single trip from :			Annual multi-trip from:		
10d	£14.70	£13.23	Adult	£51.45	£46.31
15d	£15.75	£14.18	Couple	£78.75	£70.88
31d	£24.15	£21.74	Family	£82.95	£74.66 at 10/02

10% discount - when you book via our website link - www.greekofile.co.uk - or telephone Columbus Direct on **020 7375 0011** and quote **Greek-o-File**.

No discount on annual insurance for over 65s.

You do not have to take insurance with your tour operator, but may be asked for policy details to prove you are covered.

Greek-o-File Logos

to personalise your T-shirt, sweatshirt, vest, shorts, sundress, or other cotton item - Iron-on Greek-o-File registered trade mark logos **cyan & black** (colour as book front) seagull silhouette & name or just use the seagull
**3 logos 6x4cm (size as here) for £1.95 or larger
2 logos 9x6cm for £2.50 inc** VAT and P&P for UK.

Greek-o-File™

Additional offers for direct subscribers

Reply Form

If you would like to be **notified when future issues** are to be published,
order offer items, send a **contribution for consideration** in future books, or
recommend restaurants or Greek classes in UK, please complete this form
(or a copy) where appropriate and post with any relevant details or payment to
Greek-o-File, 4 Harvey Road, Langley, Nr Slough, Berks, SL3 8JB, UK, or contact
for more information - Tel **01753 544475**, Email **mail@greekofile.co.uk**.

Name Mr/Mrs/Ms/Miss _____

Address _____

_____

_____ Post Code _____

Tel (Day / Eve) _____

Email address _____

Where did you buy/find this book? _____

I would like:

To be notified when future Greek-o-File volumes will be available ____
If you purchased this book direct you will automatically be notified - let us know if you move.

To purchase additional copies of The Greek-o-File Vol. I @ £8 each UK ____
(£9 EU, £10 Rest of World)

To purchase Greek-o-File back issues ____no. @ £3 (or 1 @£4) UK ____
Tick or circle issues required (£3.50 EU, £4 Rest of World)

Intro - 99/1 99/2 99/3 99/4 - 00/1 00/2 00/3 00/4 - 01/1 01/2 01/3 01/4 - 02/1 02/2
FREE Greek-o-<u>File</u> and dividers if all 15 purchased (UK only), or 15 for price of 14.

To purchase Greek-o-File logos, Ectaco Electronic Translators or **other offers** ____

I enclose an article/ item for consideration (max 3 x A4 pages, 2,000 words) ____
(2nd copy of book supplied free to contributors of articles of at least 1 page)

Optional Recommendations & Information:

Favourite
Greek Destination(s) Max.3 _____

UK Greek Restaurant _____

Address _____

_____ Tel. No _____

UK Greek Classes _____

Address _____

_____ Admin Tel. No _____

Age Group   Less than30 ☐   31-45 ☐   46-60 ☐   61+ ☐

Greek-o-File™ Company Reg. 3620858, VAT Reg GB 711 1751 75